Don't Cut the Grass On Sunday

*A Monday Conversation for Non-Christians &
Skeptics Alike*

written by

K. Stephen Jumper

ISBN : 978-1-970435-10-8

Published by : Ink Founders

Endorsements -

Stephen Jumper's new book, **Don't Cut the Grass on Sunday,** is written for the doubtful and curious reader. But its appeal reaches far beyond non-Christians and skeptics. Jumper addresses those wrestling with the ideas of religion, God, and the Bible, and shows how these truths relate to everyday life. The book also works well as a teaching resource for new believers and for English learners; Jumper uses simple language to introduce complex biblical truths in a non-threatening, step-by-step way. Having served for several years as a multicultural pastor, I appreciate a text that honestly and accurately presents truth in a gradual, building-block format.

Dr. Kent Oviatt, Carolina University, Winston-Salem, NC

This is a vivid introduction to the basic beliefs of the Christian life. The author uses a conversational tone that is easy and enjoyable to read. He has a heartfelt desire for non-believers to be introduced to Jesus. I, myself, was changed by his enthusiastic faith in God and sharing of the Bible when I was a teenager.

Carla Long, sister of the author

Pastoral Care Assistant, Hunter Street Baptist Church, Birmingham, AL.

"Thank you, Steve Jumper, for boldly challenging us all to be a part of God's Great Commission!" This book is a breath of fresh air. With so many searching for answers, it's refreshing to have such a resource pointing them to the ultimate source of hope, Jesus Christ. You'll certainly want to share this with friends and family."

Stu Epperson Jr., Author, Last Words of Jesus

President, Truth Network, Winston-Salem, NC.

You will find this book to be easy to read. You will not be confused by the use of big theological words, statements, and doctrines. You will find comfort in knowing that Stephen Jumper puts you at ease as he challenges your thoughts concerning a more relational way of leading non-believers in their discovery of God. His attempt at addressing the Christian life is deep and profound as he presents a "straightforward" approach. He uses direct questions to probe the thought process of non-believers while laying out in this book a body of work that does not confuse, but rather clarifies. He has spent an enormous amount of time and energy to make the case, which we all should consider, as we put forth the Gospel Message to impact the lives of those who need it the most.

Boots Hubbard, Director of Missions

Paluxy Baptist Association, Granbury, Texas

Dedicated to –

- my grandparents, Julian Thomas (J.T.) & Marvelle Banks, for passing along biblical values to both me and my sister Carla.

- my mother, Norma Rae (Banks) Jumper, for teaching me the love for books and reading.

- my Sr. High English teacher, Mr. B.C. Crawford, for teaching me the passion for writing… and to write about anything.

Table Of Contents

Chapter 9

Chapter 10

Introduction

Is This Book for You?

Does the Bible really teach that you cannot cut your grass on Sunday? Are you a non-Christian, described on the front cover, who thinks that Christianity is a stringent system of rules that makes life no fun? *Would you consider yourself a non-believer or just a skeptic? Is it at all possible to know if God exists?*

In the following pages, I have attempted to share with you some of the most important parts of what the Bible says as plainly as possible. I am assuming that you know little or nothing about the Bible and about Christianity in general. My goal is to give you information that you do not have or know. Christianity is extremely misunderstood these days, and given how overwhelmed our society is with information because of technological advances like social media, the Bible is often mischaracterized and frankly, downright lied about.

Even though you may know little about the Bible and Christianity, have you ever wanted to find a straightforward explanation without all the "churchy" approaches? If this even remotely describes you, then this book may be right for you.

For those of you reading this book who may have some knowledge of the Bible and may even be a Christian, I hope that you will discover something that you did not know or be enlightened by a less theological and academic approach. Perhaps you will be able to use this book to simply start a conversation with your non-Christian friends. In any case, for the rest of the book, I will be addressing the reader under the assumption that they are a non-Christian and know little about the Bible.

Chapters 1 and 2 are all about you, the non-Christian, non-believer, or skeptic. Let's consider where your unbelief may fit, and why you do not believe, or do believe the things you do. Before I go too far into details, Chapter 3 will give you a few basics that will provide you with some groundwork and perspective for the rest of the book. The chapter entitled *"It Starts with the First Book"* will cover notable events in the book of Genesis. This chapter starts with the account of creation and continues with the establishment of the Jewish people as a nation. It continues with the second book of the Bible, called Exodus, and covers Israel's flight from Egypt and entry into the Promised Land. I will provide an overview of the tribes of Israel, their initial rulers, and their subsequent downfall. In the chapter entitled *"What about this Jesus"*, I have summarized major aspects of the life and ministry of Jesus. I talk about why Jesus came, and His message of the Good News called the Gospel.

I would be remiss if I did not share the personal story behind the title, *Don't Cut the Grass on Sunday*. You will get a glimpse into my personal life. It is part of the reason that I hope to make this book conversational. Our "Monday conversation" is meant to be just that, conversational and not so academic. I will share what Jesus has to say about something like cutting the grass on Sunday. You may be surprised.

Since you may have questions about what the Christian church is all about, I have included a chapter that will highlight important points in church history. We will explore some essential spiritual beliefs and possible, or not so possible, next steps for you as the reader. Steps like sticking with not believing in God or just finding out more. In the back of the book, I have included a list of the books of the Bible, the Ten Commandments, explanations of select Bible parables, notable Bible characters, as well as some important Bible passages.

I have kept quotes from the Bible to a minimum in the body of the book and consolidated that type of information in the back intentionally. You may choose to start with the chapters that sound the most interesting. Parts of the book can simply be used for reference and certainly accessed more than one time.

In any case, I would love to hear from you. Your thoughts and feedback would be confidential. You can reach me personally on my website at

https://www.dontcutthegrassonsunday.com.

Chapter 1

If Not Christian, Then What?

I believe wrapped up in the term non-Christian, there may be many definitions that describe you or someone who picks up this book out of curiosity to explore this topic. There are different terms to describe non-Christians. These terms have various meanings and can mean different things to different people. Everyone is unique. And while I am going to list various categories of non-Christians, please understand that I recognize there can be many variations. Other descriptions of the term non-Christian could include, but are certainly not limited to the following:

a. Non-Believer/Apathetic/Non-Religious

b. Atheist

c. Agnostic

d. Skeptic

e. Higher power believer

f. Some belief in a God

g. Belief in another God, religion like Buddhism, Hinduism, Islam

h. Christian believer before but fell away.

Do any of these describe you? What category of non-Christian would you consider yourself? In the next chapter, I will address unbelief and the reasons why a person may not believe. However, let me start by briefly addressing the categories above.

Non-believers are a general category for the term non-Christians. I believe someone would choose to describe themselves this way because it is broad and less specific. It is an easy category without going into a lot of detail. Maybe someone would describe themselves this way because they have not been exposed to church or the Bible very much. They may simply know little about Christianity and just have not taken the time to find out. Perhaps this person does not really think about spiritual things that much. With our busy lifestyles these days and all the distractions the world has to offer, it is easy for a person simply to be apathetic about Christianity or any other belief system, for that matter. THIS BOOK IS WRITTEN FOR YOU, THE NON-BELIEVER.

An atheist is a person who does not believe in the existence of a supreme being, a higher power, or that there is a God. God does not exist! I have asked people who say they don't believe in the existence of God whether they believe in Heaven or Hell. When they said they did not believe in either one of these, my question was, "What do you think happens when a person dies?" The most common answer I have heard was, "When you're dead, you're dead" or "Nothing happens." While they did not describe themselves as an atheist, based on these answers, I would say they were an atheist. THIS BOOK IS WRITTEN FOR YOU, THE ATHEIST.

An agnostic is someone who believes that it is impossible to know one way or another whether God exists. This person simply believes it is beyond humanity to know the things that exist or don't exist in the universe. While I am not sure that I've talked to many people who would call themselves agnostic, I am going to guess that an agnostic would say that the Bible cannot be a reliable source for us to know that God exists. I am going to guess, too, that God in the form of the Holy Spirit cannot possibly help us to prove the existence of God. THIS BOOK IS WRITTEN FOR YOU, THE AGNOSTIC!

Later in the book, in the chapter entitled "Basics before the Basics," I will address how the Bible and the Holy Spirit are essential resources for Christians.

Also, while people may not categorize themselves as agnostic, they may agree with the agnostic that the Bible, much less the Holy Spirit, is NOT a reliable source to understand the existence of God. I just want to be sure to acknowledge that you don't have to be considered an agnostic to doubt the Bible and the Holy Spirit as reliable resources for Christians. THIS BOOK IS WRITTEN FOR YOU, THOSE WHO BELIEVE YOU CAN'T RELY ON THE BIBLE.

Are you skeptical about the Bible and Christianity? Would you describe yourself as a doubter? Do you see or even believe in some things about Christianity, but are simply skeptical? Do you question Christianity to the point that you cannot possibly bring yourself to make up your mind? Do you know some "stuff" about the Bible but waiver on believing that it could actually be true? THIS BOOK IS WRITTEN FOR YOU, THE SKEPTIC.

Maybe you are not a Christian, but you have some belief or sense somehow that a higher power exists in the universe. You do not know how you came to feel that way, but for now, you are satisfied just believing in something higher than yourself.

If this describes you and we are having a conversation, I will ask you about your level of experience with Christianity, the church, and the Bible. Where do you think this belief in a higher power comes from? Do you believe more than beyond this higher power? Have you tried to explore or research more information? Have you wanted to know some basics about Christianity to compare it to this belief in a higher power? THIS BOOK IS WRITTEN FOR YOU, THOSE WHO BELIEVE IN A HIGHER POWER.

I have had people tell me that they did believe in a God, but that was about it. Some even told me they believe in the God of the Bible, but that is where their beliefs stopped. They even seemed familiar with the God of the Bible, but did not know much beyond the fact that God created the universe, and that God was involved with the Jewish nation. The folks that I talked to, like this, had many questions for me and wanted to know more, but others were not interested in going beyond their belief in God. If this describes you and you have read this far, then please know, THIS BOOK IS WRITTEN FOR YOU, THOSE WHO HAVE A SENSE THAT THERE IS SOME GOD OUT THERE.

Do you believe in God, but it is not the God of the Bible? Do you practice another religion like Buddhism, Hinduism, Islam, or something entirely different? Have you ever explored what the Bible says and compared your current faith or spirituality to what the Bible teaches? THIS BOOK IS WRITTEN FOR YOU, THOSE WHO PRACTICE A DIFFERENT RELIGION.

Finally, there are those who understood Christianity and knew lots about the Bible. They even called themselves Christians for a time, but for assorted reasons, stopped believing and gave up on their faith in the God of the Bible. I want to acknowledge that there are many reasons that people "fall away" from the Christian faith and Christian way of life. I will not explore these reasons here, but I want to acknowledge that if you are in this category, I hear you and appreciate the fact that you would have the courage to revisit what this book may have to offer you. You are one of the reasons I have taken a different approach to sharing these Christian basics and what the Bible says. THIS BOOK IS WRITTEN FOR YOU, THE ONCE BELIEVER.

Any one of you who could fall into one of the categories above might be wondering, why would I write such a book? In speaking with people who fall into these various categories, I am enthusiastic to provide information at its most basic level of what Christianity is and what the Bible teaches. I do not think someone has sat down and thought through how to provide basic Christian beliefs and Bible knowledge in its most straightforward way. For people who do not know much about the Bible and have little or no experience with Christianity, I want to provide some fundamental information that is written as plainly as possible. This is one of the main motivations for me to author this book.

Christianity is often highly misunderstood and propagandized. Its distinct doctrines are often taken out of context, dramatized, and villainized. This is another motivation for me to take a different approach.

Some of my most valued conversations have been with non-believers at all levels. The key to this was to find non-Christians who had the fortitude to sit down and have a conversation about what they didn't believe, and what they did believe. Of course, this is a two-way street. Personally, I had to get to a point (maturity level) where I could calmly and rationally have that conversation. Once I did, the conversations with non-believers were substantive, healthy, and fun. These types of conversations enhanced our relationship. Conversations with non-believers have encouraged me to write this book.

Also, for those who could not sit down and discuss their non-Christianity with a believer, I wanted to give them a guideline of Christian basics and information about the Bible. In this way, they would have the information they needed to talk to their Christian friends. This led me to outline this style of book.

Finally, am I just another one of those crazy Christians who want to change people and convert everyone to the Christian way of thinking? I am a Christian, and later I will share my personal testimony with you. You will learn that I have a lifelong Christian background, even though there was a brief period of time when I did not focus on it. Just to make sure I provide full disclosure, I have traveled around the world on Christian mission trips telling others about my belief and faith.

So, am I trying to convert you? Here is the truth of the matter: I am not the one who converts people. My desire is simply to give you the basics. You may well end up being more comfortable with what you believe now. Even so, I enjoy sharing my story and my faith. However, the God I believe in from the Bible, through HIS Holy Spirit, is the one who convicts and converts. While a person who does not believe in God may come to be a Christian because of this book, my main motivation is what I have stated previously. I am motivated to do this in a way that cuts down on all the Bible language, "church talk," and complex Christian concepts but provides more summary explanations of what the Bible says. I have provided various Bible passages and verses to give you experience and a sense of exactly what the Bible says. While it is impossible to explain what the Bible says without showing you actual excerpts from the Bible, I have tried to minimize the number of Bible passages throughout the body of the book and paraphrase thoughts to make it easier to understand. I have consolidated most of the more direct Bible information in the back of the book. In doing so, I hope that you will use the information in the back of the book as a resource and refer to it more than once.

I will tell you now that at the end of the book, I will go into how a person becomes a Christian. Part of understanding basic Christian concepts involves knowing how someone goes from not being a Christian to becoming a Christian. If you choose to read that part and stay solid in not believing in God, at least you will be able to discuss that if it comes up in a conversation. Believe me, even the way a Christian becomes a Christian can be controversial. One of the biggest failures for many Christians is not sharing how one becomes a Christian. It would be like me telling you about how great my golf membership is at the country club, but never telling you the membership qualifications and how to join.

One thing that I would like to encourage you to ask yourself is, how convinced am I of my unbelief? How committed are you to not believing in God? At the beginning of the book of Revelation, God is confronting seven churches. He tells one of the churches that they are a "lukewarm" church, that they are neither hot nor cold. He then continues by saying that because they are neither hot nor cold, and because they are "lukewarm," He will "spew" them from His mouth. These are harsh and descriptive words.

I believe what God is saying not only to this church, but to people everywhere, is that it is better to be committed and convinced one way or another of their beliefs and actions. *I believe God is saying, "Take a side," either believe or do not believe.* The ones that are in the middle and are wavering, languid, and even "wishy-washy" will surely be rejected by God (if He exists, of course). So, I am motivated to share what the Bible says in a way that does motivate you about what you believe in or do not believe in. I encourage you that if you do not believe in God, own it, and understand why it is that you believe the way you do. I have been spurred on in this way as well to author this book.

With all this in mind, I hope and trust that you feel comfortable that I have been straight up with you. Also, I hope that you have a better understanding of whether this book is right for you. My desire is that this book would be a refreshing approach.

Chapter 2

So, You Don't Believe

So, you don't believe? What is it that you don't believe? Does God exist in your mind? Do you even believe in "a" God? Or is it a "higher power" that you believe in?

Have you simply decided that all the things around us just evolved over billions of years, without the involvement of a creator? Is science the thing that holds it all together? Does evolution explain that the universe has been around for millions and billions of years? *Can I encourage you before you dive deeper into the next chapters that you will stop and think through exactly what you do not believe, and even what you do believe?*

We all hear lots of things these days. Our world is proliferated with more information than we ever thought possible. Brought along by the advancements in technology, human beings are exposed to and being asked to process more information than ever intended. This information overload in technology threatens our ability to maintain a healthy mental and emotional state. Now, with the advent of artificial intelligence and supercomputing, we will all see and experience things in our lifetime that we did not think would be possible or could have ever imagined.

What are your sources of information? Just like politics on television today, there are many opinionated voices. How credible are the voices to which you are listening? Has your source been vetted? Do other sources support and collaborate with one another? These are extremely important questions in a world where everyone seems to be an expert.

Do you realize that the Bible is available to more people around the world today than ever before? Also, there are more supporting documents that have been discovered, and there are an ever-growing number of commentaries and analyses. Certainly, this is the case in America today, yet we (both Christians and non-Christians) do not access and utilize this information enough to fully commit to what we believe.

Would you believe that Christians hear things about the Bible and about God that are not true, but they believe it anyway? I know because I used to be one of those people, particularly in my early days of becoming a Christian, and even after I became a Christian. I have talked to many non-Christians who share things that they have heard and have "bought into." They believe things without doing the necessary research to find out the truth. This is a dangerous place for any of us to be, regardless of whether we are speaking about Christianity or any other subject.

This is just a small amount of reasoning as to why I really encourage you to do some self-examination of your own beliefs or disbeliefs prior to reading further. For example, what was your "upbringing" like, your childhood? What did your parents, family, guardians, and friends believe? What schools did you attend, and what did they teach you?

What area or region of the country did you grow up in? Growing up in the Northeast is much different than growing up in the South. Growing up in Texas is much different than growing up in Washington State. From California to the Carolinas, we live in a diverse country consisting of many distinct cultures and belief systems. While this diversity can be a beautiful thing (God-given, for that matter), it can have its challenges when we base our beliefs on false information or lack of the truth.

What factors have affected what you think? What factors have affected what you believe? I really hope that you will do some self-reflection even while you are reading through this book.

Just so you know, I grew up and have lived most of my life in the South, the Southeast. However, I am well-traveled across the United States and have lived and stayed in a few interesting places. Also, I have had the benefit of traveling around the world, fortunately. Traveling outside the United States will give you a unique perspective for sure.

Would you believe that I attended a Christian school in the 1970s, and they taught me evolution in science class? As an adult, I look back and can objectively see how it conflicted with my Christian upbringing. I did not know it at the time, but I was really confused! I did not even realize that the various ideas and concepts that I was being taught were counterintuitive!

One of the crazy things that I was taught back in the 1970s was a theory that Ernst Haeckel had developed about when an embryo is first developing in the early stages of pregnancy. He theorized that the embryo was transformed into a fish stage with gill slits and went through other evolutionary stages until it became human. This theory seemed to imply that the universe was determining if the human baby growing inside the womb was even going to be human. As a vulnerable and impressionable seventh grader, I believed this theory for some time. The theory was short-lived, though, and Ernst Haeckel admitted that his claim was fraudulent.[1]

So, where are you with what you believe, and looking even deeper, are you comfortable with where you are with what you believe? What if you wrote down what you did not believe, and even

---

[1] Ken Ham, *The Lie: Evolution/Millions of Years* (Green Forest, AR: Master Books, 2012), 147.

some things you might believe? Here are a few thoughts to get started:

➤ I don't believe in anything.

➤ I don't believe that God exists (I'm assuming you mean the God of the Bible).

➤ I don't believe that Jesus existed, and the Holy Spirit is out of the question.

➤ I don't believe what the Bible says.

➤ I don't believe in going to church.

➤ I don't believe in Heaven or Hell.

➤ I believe, "when you are dead, you are dead."

➤ I believe we came from nothing, and we will go back to nothing.

➤ I believe there is a higher power.

➤ I believe there is an afterlife (Heaven, Hell, reincarnation, another dimension).

➤ I believe in God, but Jesus is what I have a problem with.

➤ Jesus was just a great teacher and prophet.

➤ The Bible was written by fallible men and is full of errors and contradictions.

➤ I believe the church is corrupt.

I am sure this list is not all-encompassing, but do any of these describe you? I am sure you have other things that you could write down. In any case, my goal is that we get off on the "right foot" and get a good start before we dive into some basic Christian concepts.

What about Truth?

In addition to starting with some reflection about what you believe or do not believe about God, the Bible, etc., what are your thoughts about "TRUTH?" Do you believe that absolute truth exists, or is truth relative? Can everyone decide what "their" truth is? How does "their" truth affect others? How does it affect you? Simply, is there "NO ABSOLUTE TRUTH?" If so, are you sure about that "ABSOLUTELY?"

The concept of understanding "TRUTH" plays a vital role in working through the basics of Christianity. True Christians rely on the Bible to learn, understand, and accept the "Truth" it teaches. Predominantly, Jesus, in the first four books of the New Testament called the Gospels (Matthew, Mark, Luke, and John), defines "Truth." Jesus actually states that, "He is the Truth." He is conveying that not only is He "Truth" in the form of a man, but that His words are "Truth." In the book of John 14:6 (NKJV),

[6] Jesus said to him, "I am the way, the truth, and the life. No one comes to the Father except through Me."

Also, in the book of John 1:1-5, 14 (NKJV):

> [1] In the beginning was the Word, and the Word was with God, and the Word was God. [2] He was in the beginning with God. [3] All things were made through Him, and without Him nothing was made that was made. [4] In Him was life, and the life was the light of men. [5] And the light shines in the darkness, and the darkness did not comprehend it. [14] And the Word became flesh and dwelt among us, and we beheld His glory, the glory as of the only begotten of the Father, full of grace and truth.

These seven verses are core to the foundation of Christian belief. Jesus defines Himself as truth, meaning that both His teachings and He are truth. When John writes, "in the beginning," he is referring to Jesus' existence at the time of creation, and that He is the "Word." He is saying that He is the Word of God in the flesh, all things were created through Him, and that He is light.

I wanted to introduce you to this basic Christian teaching as you continue to explore what you do and do not believe. While you do not have to understand it now (Christians revisit and study this constantly), it is important to contrast our conversation regarding unbelief and not being a Christian.

Also, throughout this book, Bible passages are included as references to support explanations about the basics of Christianity. As mentioned earlier, I have tried to minimize these references in the body of the book and paraphrase as much as possible.

A segment of non-Christians and skeptics suggests that Christians cannot use the Bible as evidence for the existence of God. They will say that it was written by men, is fallible, and unreliable. From a Christian worldview, this is impossible. As we will discuss in the next chapter, the Bible is the foundation of Christianity. It is what Christians stand on. It is where Christians base their truth. So, given this fact, where do non-Christians base their truth? If they do not believe in absolute truth, what and where is the foundation of anything they believe? What would you say is the foundation of what you believe?

Common Non-Christian Viewpoints

There are many viewpoints held by non-Christians, non-believers, atheists, agnostics, and skeptics alike. While there are too many viewpoints to cover completely, let us consider a few before we dive into some Christian basics in the next chapter. Here is a list to get us started:[2]

- There is no evidence of God's existence.

- If God created the universe, who created God?

- God is not all-powerful if there is something He cannot do. God cannot lie; therefore, God is not all-powerful.

---

[2]Eric Hyde, "Top 10 Most Common Atheist Arguments, and Why They Fail," Eric Hyde's Blog, March 21, 2014.

- Believing in God is the same as believing in the Tooth Fairy or Santa Claus.

- Christianity arose from ancient and ignorant people who lacked science.

- Christians only believe because they were born in a Christian culture. If they were born in India, they would be Hindu.

- The Gospel does not make sense. God was mad at humans, so He tortured His own Son because of His pathological anger.

- History is full of mother-child messiah cults, trinity godheads. Christianity is a myth like other stories.

- The God of the Bible is evil. He allows suffering and death.

- Evolution answers the question of creation. Christianity is another ignorant ancient myth.

In reality, there has never been more evidence of the existence of God. Just like with written resources, advances in science and technology are available to address the list above. Also, archaeological discoveries continue to support the claims of the Bible. By discussing "non-Christianity" before we dive into the basics of Christianity, my goal is to recognize and acknowledge the possible perspective of you, the reader. I am sure there are many who will read these first two chapters and conclude they do not fit any of these descriptions of non-belief. Regardless, again, my goal is to provide the reader with basic information about Christianity and the Bible, so that they can be better informed. Perhaps with this information, they will be able to research more and even enhance their conversations with their non-Christian and Christian friends alike.

Chapter 3

Basics Before the Basics

Before diving into all the basics about Christianity, I think it is fair to start with a few concepts that will help make processing the rest of the book easier. I could call them helpful prerequisites.

The purpose of starting with these first few concepts is to help you understand where believing in God starts. Most Christian books I read make an incredible leap and assume the audience has a background in Christianity or church experience.

An important ground rule to make clear: this book is about educating the reader and making knowledge available to them. Also, let me be clear, I am not trying to persuade you to my way of thinking. It is not me who persuades on a topic like this. As we will discuss throughout this book, it is God, the Holy Spirit, who draws a person and influences them.

The information contained here about the Bible is not my opinion, nor is it my attempt to project or put my views on you. Please note that the explanations I provide throughout the book, particularly those when it comes to the interpretations of the Parables, are based on my education, spiritual journey, and life experience. You may see a comment or opinion or two on certain things. Who could help themselves, right? But I do not have the need to convince you of anything or change your mind. We all have free will. We are all responsible for ourselves and should be fully capable of making our own decisions. We should all know, too, that we must live with the consequences of those decisions as well.

Hopefully, I will accomplish the goal of providing you with the plainest language to simply give you the knowledge you have not had before. With this knowledge, maybe you will be able to begin a conversation that would lead to an even better understanding of what the Bible teaches.

Today, our culture is more divided than ever on what they believe, particularly when it comes to God, faith, family, and yes, politics. We all base our own judgments on the lens through which we look. Again, if you have little or no experience with the Bible, then the lens you look through is simply missing basic information that would help you openly discuss your non-belief or disbelief with someone. Perhaps you will be in a better position to simply understand a different viewpoint or possibly preserve a close relationship with a friend or family member.

I have attempted to minimize Christian jargon and religiosity. Most Christian books are filled with Bible verses that dive into deep concepts that can be confusing and require quite a bit of research. I wanted to provide the basic Bible verses to explain the most basic concepts without the need for long "theological" (a fancy religious word meaning "to study God") discussions. This is just a starting point, and the idea is that, for someone with little or no reference point, a reference point can be established. With just minimal foundational knowledge, believe me, there is no limit to what can be researched, discussed, and written about.

Also, may I suggest it is not necessary to read this book in order? You may want to jump to chapters that sound more interesting to you or the chapters that might discuss an area of Christianity that you have been curious about. There are books that you should definitely read from beginning to end, but I suggest that this book might not be that way for you.

This book is not comprehensive of Christianity and what the Bible says. It is intended for you to get the core information you could use to answer some questions you have about the Christian faith. Believe me, people cannot spend a lifetime absorbing all the data and information on Christianity and the Bible. In our capitalistic society, Christianity has truly become an industry.

Does it surprise you that I said that? Well, hopefully, that is just a piece of plain talk that you will find here. You see, one of the problems in our culture today is that Christianity has gotten convoluted, and it has gotten misrepresented. There are two simple reasons—both Christians and non-Christians. And to me, it is Christians who are mostly to blame.

Many times, I have heard people talk about their bad experiences, hurt, and pain over a fellow Christian or church and how they were treated. In most cases, this is a big problem in our church today. I could go on and on regarding how the church has drifted from what it was intended to be, but I'll touch on that in a later chapter. If you are a person who has had an unpleasant experience dealing with Christian people or the Christian church in general, then this book is for you.

Many times, I have heard committed non-believers use misinformation, misstate, or simply have no information to discuss Christianity. They are simply unable to substantiate even their own beliefs. If this describes you, and if you can have an open mind about information that might be overwhelming, I believe the information contained in the following pages will help you to sort out and substantiate your thoughts and beliefs.

But again, this is not about me proving anything. While what I may tell you constitutes some proof, you by no means need to take it or accept it as any proof. The idea is to make the information precise and as simple as possible to understand.

So, before we begin, here is your opportunity to put the book down and stop reading. I offer this because I do realize that I need to build a certain amount of trust with you so that you keep a slightly open mind with what it is I choose to share with you and how I share it. Hopefully, it is just the right amount of information to keep you invested in finding out more. I hope you appreciate the approach!

The following four Bible basics about Christianity are essential to building upon other Christian beliefs. While you will not agree nor fully understand these concepts, it is important that you are aware that these will build upon the rest of what the Bible teaches. For the interim, just know that they are a "given" to most Christians.

Basic #1 – God is ONE God in THREE Persons referred to as The Trinity

So, please do not get discouraged when you read, "there is one God, but He is in the form of three persons called the Trinity." Would you be surprised to know that most Christians struggle with the concept of "The Trinity"? Many Christian beliefs are difficult for ANYONE to understand. The idea here is that you just get started and gain some initial knowledge that will help make the rest of this book make more sense.

While Christians believe there is truly ONE God, God exists in the form of God the Father, God the Son, and God the Holy Spirit. Christians believe that this has been true for all eternity. Eternity being without a beginning and without an end.

God is outside of time as we know it. He must be, to be God. He did not have a beginning, and He does not have an end. God is all-knowing, all-powerful, and is "our" past, present, and future. He has always been and will always be. He made all things, sustains all things, and is in control of all things.

He is a God of Order, a God of Love, a God of Justice, and a God of Forgiveness (Grace). At this point, you may be saying, "That's not what I have heard or know of about God." Why is there so much suffering in the world, then? Why doesn't He just save us all from the terrible things that happen in the world? In Chapter 9, I will be addressing some of these questions by recounting the story of Job (pronounced "Jobe") from the Bible, regarding how God deals with Satan and evil in the world.

These questions are great! And these questions have answers based on the Christian faith. However, these questions are beyond where we are heading in our study of basic Christian beliefs. There are so many scholars who have addressed questions like these. Simply put, these questions are not intended to be answered here, but they are an example of how, when you are introduced to Christianity, there is much more to be learned.

So why three Gods that make up ONE God? Would an acceptable answer be that part of me "can't possibly fully understand it myself?" Here's a way that helps me think about it. Whether you are a man or a woman, you are a son or a daughter. At the same time, if you have married, you are a husband or wife. If you have children, then you are a father and a mother as well. Do you have brothers and sisters? You can play all these separate roles simultaneously without compromising who you are as an individual. Also, in these distinct roles, you have varying relationships and responsibilities.

While this explanation is rudimentary in nature, personally, for me, this is a key in understanding who God really is. However, it is important to understand that while God exists in three distinct persons, God is ONE God. In the book of Deuteronomy, chapter 6, verse 4, **"Hear, O Israel: The Lord our God, the LORD is one!"** And in the book of John, chapter 17, verse 21, **Jesus prayed, "that they all may be one, as You, Father, are in Me, and I in You; that they also may be one in Us, that the world may believe that You sent Me."** Jesus was praying for his disciples. These are deep spiritual Bible passages that give us insight into the Trinity.

Can Christians ever fully understand the concept of the Trinity? I am pretty sure the answer to that question is a resounding

"No," but through faith, Christians can still trust that God is who He says He is.

When I think about God, my Father, I am drawn to think first about my earthly father. Fortunately, I was blessed (Christian word alert) to have a good relationship with my own father. He was a good man. In other words, I had an example. However, God the Father in Heaven is much, much more than that. I know this "Heavenly Father" from what I read in the Bible, by prayer, and through my ever-changing spiritual relationship with Him.

Would you believe that the Bible tells us that we can actually call God our Father in Heaven, "Daddy"? In the Bible, in the book of Romans, the author of that book, Paul, writes that we have a Father who can sympathize with us and that we cry out to Him like a child would call to their earthly father, "Daddy." And actually, to quote the verse is to say, **"we cry Abba,"** which in Greek can be translated as "Daddy." For me, it is great comfort to know I have that kind of relationship with what I believe is the Creator of the universe.

Now let us talk about Jesus, the Son of God. The Bible tells us that Jesus, God the Son, was with God the Father in Heaven. In the book of Philippians, chapter 2, the Bible says that He did not count Himself equal to God but chose to come to earth in the form of a man to save the world from their sin of disobedience and rebellion.

The Bible tells us that He "emptied Himself" and came to earth as both God and Man. To put it simply, "emptied Himself" means that He left His own Glory and deity in Heaven to come to earth in the form of a human being.

At the very core of Christianity is the belief, based on what the Bible tells us, that Jesus was born physically just like you and I were born. The difference is how He was conceived. The Bible tells us that He was conceived by the Holy Spirit through the Virgin Mary, which takes us to the third person of the Trinity, the Holy Spirit. God, the Holy Spirit, is God's Spirit that is provided for us to be a guide and to help us understand and know God.

The Bible describes the role of the Holy Spirit as a counselor, comforter, intercessor, and one who convicts us. Beyond these basic roles, there is much more that the Holy Spirit provides. In summary, the Bible tells us that it was God the Father who dealt with people before Jesus came. Jesus came from Heaven and lived on earth for approximately thirty-three years before returning to His throne in Heaven. After Jesus, God the Father sent His Holy Spirit to dwell among men on earth, and the Bible teaches us that He is here with us this very day.

Basic #2 – Two Main Sources of Christian Beliefs: The Bible and the Holy Spirit

To gain an initial perspective, non-believers and skeptics should understand that Christians gain their beliefs from two main sources: the Bible and the Holy Spirit.

This is not to say that exposure to family, friends, and the church are not influences, and sometimes even main drivers of Christian belief. However, when it comes to growth and maturity as a Christian over a lifetime, it is the Bible and God the Holy Spirit that make it possible.

When a Christian reaches a certain level of maturity in their belief system, they understand that the Bible is one of the main reasons why they believe what they believe. To know what the Bible says and to understand its purpose is truly foundational to being a well-grounded Christian.

The Bible is divided into two parts: the Old Testament and the New Testament. The Old Testament consists of 39 different books and covers the time period from the creation of the earth until the birth of Jesus (around 6000 B.C. to 5 B.C.). The New Testament consists of 27 books and covers the time period from the birth of Jesus, ending with the book of John (5 B.C. to 100 A.D.). The last book of the Bible, called Revelation, was written then, but it covers an unknown time period when the earth, as we know it, will end and there will be a New Heaven and a New Earth (sometime yet to come).

While the Bible is divided into the Old and New Testaments, consisting of 66 individual books, it is one story. You could think of them as chapters, but they were written so that they could actually stand alone. Some of them are letters, while others are poetry and wisdom. Also, there is more than one human author. Approximately forty different men on three different continents are considered to have written these 66 different books. They all come together to tell one story.

This collection of 66 books put into one book called the Bible came about in the 4th century. Initially, the Old Testament was written in Hebrew, and the New Testament was written in Greek. Martin Luther, whom you will read about later, translated the Bible from Latin into German. The Bible was translated into what is known today as the King James Bible in 1611. Today, there are many translations. More commonly used translations of the Bible are New King James, New International Version, English Standard Version, and many more. The important thing to know about translations is whether it is a version that is a word-for-word translation or a paraphrased version. Hebrew and Greek are best understood by a word-for-word translation. Most of the Bible verses quoted in this book are taken from the New King James unless otherwise noted.[3]

While some forty different men wrote the Bible, Christians consider that there is truly one author of the Bible, and that is God. The Bible says that God inspired these men to write His word and that "scripture is Spirit-breathed."

I know many non-believers and non-Christians want to discount the Bible. I have even had non-believing friends tell me that if we were going to have a conversation, I could not use the Bible as a reference. The main reason I was told that I couldn't use the Bible is that it was written by men. And yes, the Bible was written by men, but there is an answer to that question as well, and a deeper reason Christians trust the Bible. The Bible teaches that the words of the Bible came from God, not men. These men were inspired by God's Holy Spirit, and the Bible even goes so far as to say that the words of the Bible were "God-breathed." Christians trust and read the Bible to learn and get to know God.

As Christians read the Bible, they believe, and frankly, they will testify, that the reason they can understand what it says is that God the Holy Spirit helps them. Does this mean that they understand everything they read? "Absolutely not." When Christians say that the

---

[3]Paul Enns, _The Moody Handbook of Theology_ (Chicago: Moody Publishers, 1989), 175.

Holy Spirit helps them, they mean that they see themselves in the story and gain a better understanding and insight into who God is and His will for their lives. They are given the foundation of truth that they can use throughout their life to navigate the struggles of the world around them.

I have heard it said that the Bible is a tremendously complex book, but in other instances, I have heard that it has a simple message. Could you understand that both may be true?

The Bible is essential to Christianity, whether you agree, disagree, accept, or reject all of what it says. Hopefully, it's a relief to you that I am not going to go into "all" of what the Bible says and "all" of what you may think are some of the craziest ideas and messages. The Bible is foundational to Christianity, and to understand some Christian basics, you need to know a few things about the book and a few things about what it says.

Basic #3 – It Boils Down to FAITH

What in your life have you had to do or believe and simply take it on faith? Have you had to take a step of faith in your life when faced with different situations? How about marriage? I recall (both times) the decision to marry came down to a step of faith. Having my first child and driving away from the hospital, not knowing what I was doing, was a step of faith. Taking a new job and moving to a new city was a step of faith.

These examples of faith should help you think about your own life when faith played a role. However, the faith to believe that there is a God and that He loves you and wants a personal relationship with you goes much deeper. Faith is one of the most basic things about the Christian life. You could say it is foundational.

Did you consider that faith does not come in an instant? Later, we will talk about the experience and how someone becomes a believer, but faith is something that is developed over time and something that takes time.

What is faith? Faith is walking without seeing, but then you start to understand, you start to see glimpses of evidence, and more faith comes. You start to believe, and more faith comes. You start to trust, and more faith comes. You start to walk by faith and not by sight (as the Bible says), and more faith comes. With each decision that you take by faith and experience insight and success, more faith comes.

This is how faith in God works. First, *faith comes by hearing, and hearing comes by the word of God (as the Bible says).* In some instances, the word of God comes by reading the Bible, and other times the word of God comes through another person. Just like you are reading this book now, the word of God is coming to you. It is NOT that you are reading the Bible, but it is like I am standing in front of you and telling you what the Bible says.

Christians who "share their faith" and their story (their personal testimony) bring the word of God to non-believers, non-Christians, and even Christians alike.

Again, faith is something that Christians develop as they learn more about God by reading their Bible and relying on the Holy Spirit to help them understand and know God better each day. It is a daily walk.

Basic #4 – The Bible Teaches That There is a Heaven and There is a Hell

While many people want to talk about Heaven, most people certainly do not want to talk about Hell. The Bible teaches that after a person dies, their soul lives on in one of two places: Heaven or Hell. While I will not pretend to be an expert on what these two places are like, I can tell you with certainty that a person will be with God eternally in Heaven, or a person will be eternally separated from God in Hell. Is it too simple to believe that we are eternal beings? Is it too simple to believe that if we die, the lights go out, and it is over?

Let me share with you two passages from the Bible that talk about Heaven. The first passage is Jesus talking to His disciples. His ministry was ending, and He was telling them that He had to go away. So, in this passage from the book of John, chapter 14, verses 1-3, Jesus comforts His disciples.

¹ "Let not your heart be troubled; you believe in God, believe also in Me. ² In My Father's house are many mansions; if it were not so, I would have told you. I go to prepare a place for you. ³ And if I go and prepare a place for you, I will come again and receive you to Myself; that where I am, there you may be also."

In this next passage, Jesus' disciple John is recounting his visions of the future in the book of Revelation, chapter 21, verses 1-4. John sees the final day of the old earth, which has passed away, and the new earth establishing God's Kingdom. Literally, Heaven on Earth.

¹ Now I saw a new Heaven and a new earth, for the first Heaven and the first earth had passed away. Also, there was no more sea. ² Then I, John, saw the holy city, New Jerusalem, coming down out of Heaven from God, prepared as a bride adorned for her husband. ³ And I heard a loud voice from Heaven saying, "Behold, the tabernacle of God is with men, and He will dwell with them, and they shall be His people. God Himself will be with them and be their God. ⁴ And God will wipe away every tear from their eyes; there shall be no more death, nor sorrow, nor crying. There shall be no more pain, for the former things have passed away."

In summary, here are the basics before the basics. Just keep them in mind as you read further. They are underlying beliefs and will be interwoven within the rest of the basic Bible concepts and Christian beliefs.

Basic #1 – **The Trinity:** God the Father, God the Son, and God the Holy Spirit

Basic #2 – **Two Main Sources:** The Bible and the Holy Spirit

Basic #3 – **FAITH:** Believing and Acting on It

Basic #4 – **Heaven or Hell:** An Eternal Home for All

Chapter 4

It Starts with the First Book

Now, let's talk about what the Bible actually says and why it says it. The first book of the Bible is called Genesis. The first four words of Genesis are: *In the beginning, God.* At first glance, you may think that God actually had a beginning. He did not. The words "In the Beginning" refer to the beginning of time. "In the Beginning" was man's beginning, not God's.

You see, God exists outside of time. He must; otherwise, He would not be God. Although you and I exist within the confines of time, space, and matter, if God is truly God, He cannot be limited by such things. The Bible says that God is an eternal being and has always existed. He has no beginning and no end.

One key point: when the Bible refers to God here in Genesis, it actually means God as the Trinity, as mentioned in the previous chapter. God the Father, God the Son, and God the Holy Spirit are eternal with no beginning and no end. Please remember the Trinity is a hard concept for even the best Christians to understand. Without getting into additional details about the Trinity, I just wanted you to be aware that the reference to God in these first words is more than you think.

How do we know this? Later in Genesis, God uses the term US when He talks about creating man in His own image. *God says, "Let US make man in OUR own image."* God refers to Himself as US, meaning Father, Son, and Holy Spirit. We will touch on this throughout the book, but for now, I simply wanted to introduce this concept.

As a child and youth, I would look around me and ask about who made what and how certain things came to be. I was simply trying to figure out how the world worked and, by asking questions, I was hoping to get answers. If you were like me as a child, I asked my parents and family lots of questions about how the world worked. One of the questions I asked repeatedly was, "Who made this?" and "How did this get here?" When I was hearing about God for the first time and learning about Him, I was asking, "Well, who made God?" It was a tough one to get by, and it took years and decades to understand the concept of anything being infinite. Understanding that God is infinite and exists outside of what we know as time is important.

If you have this shared experience, then you can relate, but if you did not grow up asking questions about God, you may not. I still do that today, and if you have picked up this book and read it this far, I hope you will reflect on and pursue the questions that you have in order to get your own answers.

Probably the first time I began to grasp the concept was studying math and learning about negative numbers. Think of it this way. A ruler starts at zero, and if it went out to the right, there was no end to the positive numbers. Now, put another ruler to the left and imagine those same numbers going towards the negative, starting with -1, -2, and so on. In both directions, there is infinity.

Would you believe it is that way in our world and not God's world? You see, you need to remember that we are created inside of time, space, and matter. Outside of that, where God is, none of our world exists the way it does. The ruler, math, and numbers example are just one way to help explain infinity.

So, back to "In the Beginning, God." Now that you can understand that a beginning is really "our" beginning or "man's beginning," when time started, let's now focus on God. Who God is and what God is all about.

Again, God is eternal and infinite. He has always been and always will be, according to the Bible. He is all-knowing and all-powerful. In Christian circles, the words Omniscient (all-knowing), Omnipresent (present everywhere), and Omnipotent (all-powerful) are used. God is complete in Himself. He exists fully and needs nothing to make Him complete. Can you let your mind go there, that before anything existed as we know it, there was only God and His eternal being? He is only God in this way.

The Bible teaches that God is Love, Just, and Merciful. He is in control of everything. A Christian word to describe that is SOVEREIGN.

As a non-Christian, you are probably going to get tired of hearing the words "according to the Bible" and "based on what the Bible says." However, to understand what Christianity is and what Christians think, you must appreciate that a Christian's faith and beliefs are rooted in what the Bible teaches. Recall I mentioned that the two main sources of a Christian's belief are the Holy Spirit and the Bible. While I recognize that for non-Christians it is hard to understand, it is the truth. Some Christians don't even understand it.

Christians believe that the world came into existence because God spoke the words and created it. From nothing, it was God who spoke and caused creation to exist and have a beginning. *"God said."* *It is as simple as that.*

The Big Bang Theory teaches that out of nothing came something. The Big Bang teaches that out of one super explosion, the universe came to be and began to evolve. According to the Big Bang, the universe did not have a creator; it just started (out of no causal effect). The Theory of Evolution teaches that over millions and billions of years, the earth formed, and then, out of a single cell, man evolved.

The Bible tells us that God created the Heavens and the earth, and all that exists, in the matter of 6 days. The Bible teaches that God designated the seventh day as a day of rest, a Sabbath day. In general, Sabbath means rest. We will talk more about that seventh day in a later chapter. For now, let's focus on those first six days.

On Day One, God created light and separated it from the darkness. He called the light day, and the darkness He called night. On Day Two, God separated the Earth and Heaven. The Bible uses the word firmament. On Day Three, God separated the waters from the dry land. He created vegetation, plants, and fruit trees. On Day Four, God created the sun, moon, and stars, which brought forth the seasons, days, and years. On Day Five, God created living creatures in the oceans and on the earth. On Day Six, God created more animal life, and most importantly, on Day Six, God created Man.

A special note of what the Bible tells us about the creation of vegetation, plants, trees, and all living things, both animals and man: when God created these things, He created them all, "according to their kind." This is particularly important when it comes to the creation of humans. God created man and woman "according to their kind" or their species. So, in contrast to evolution, while species do evolve based on their environment, they do not evolve into other species of beings. The Bible teaches that man did not evolve from apes or any other species. He made two genders, male and female.

While you are likely to have different beliefs and viewpoints, I am simply attempting to tell you about the basis of Christianity and what the Bible says. Previously, as I have said, this book is not about persuading you differently but mainly about providing you with information you may not have known before.

Recall earlier when I said that the Bible states that God said, "Let US make man in OUR own image?" *God created the first man, and his name was Adam. God then created the first woman, and her name was Eve. According to the Bible, this was the beginning of the human race.*

This brings us to evolution's teaching that all creation, including man, evolved from a single-cell organism. At some point, that organism evolved into a monkey or ape, and at some point, over millions and billions of years, that ape evolved into man.

Whatever your thought process or beliefs, the Bible and Christianity teach that God simply spoke Adam into existence. God created Eve when He took a rib from Adam's side.

When God created the universe, the earth, and man, all were in perfect union and harmony with one another. God created man to have a relationship with Him, and there was nothing in between God and man. This was the way God intended it to be, and He desired to have a relationship with Adam and Eve and all their descendants.

God placed Adam and Eve in the Garden of Eden, where they had dominion over all things and really over all the earth. However, they were forbidden from doing one thing. They were commanded not to eat from the tree of the knowledge of good and evil, which grew in the midst of the garden.

After being tempted by Satan, Adam and Eve disobeyed God and ate from the forbidden tree. When they did, something called SIN entered the world. Sin separated man from God. You see, God is Holy and perfect and will not have any relationship to sin and what is evil.

So now we have a problem, a BIG problem if you believe there is a God. But as a non-Christian, you would not see this problem, and that is certainly understandable. Why would sin have anything to do with your life if you don't believe that the God of the Bible exists?

When Adam and Eve disobeyed God and sinned against Him, the punishment for that was death and eternal separation from God. But God, who is full of mercy and grace, had compassion upon them and did not kill them. They were removed from the Garden of Eden and had to live the rest of their lives in a sinful, destructive world.

But God still required a punishment for their sin. After all, as mentioned previously, God is a Just God. He requires justice.

While you may not completely understand the SIN problem, it is central to what comes next in the book of Genesis in the Bible. God takes the initiative and begins a process that will provide a way for sinful man to get back to his relationship with God again.

After Adam and Eve had been removed from the Garden of Eden, they began their lives having to work in a fallen world. They had two sons named Cain and Abel. Cain was a farmer, and Abel was a shepherd who herded sheep. Given the fact that the world was now a sinful place, it wasn't long before the first murder happened— and it happened between these brothers.

Cain became angry and jealous of Abel because God had respected and accepted Abel's gift of worship over Cain's. In his anger, Cain killed Abel, and this was the first recorded murder and death in the Bible.

The Bible tells us that God still had a relationship with and spoke to all of them, even after they were removed from the Garden of Eden. In fact, God cared for them. He had mercy on Cain and did not kill him. Cain lived apart from the rest of his family because of his sin against his brother Abel.

The Bible tells us the names of the generations of Adam, but does not get specific about the additional daughters that Adam and his sons must have had. Many people who are not familiar with Bible genealogy are often puzzled about how one man and one woman could populate the earth. While this question is beyond the scope of Bible basics, I did want to mention that because generations of men are mentioned in the Bible, starting with Adam, we can extrapolate that many daughters were born among these generations of men.

Noah was one of the descendants of Adam, and to give you an example of how detailed the Bible can be, here is the genealogy of Adam to Noah, along with the number of years each man lived:

- Adam lived 930 years; his son was

- Seth, who lived 807 years, his son was

- Enosh, who lived 905 years, his son was

- Cainan, who lived 910 years, his son was

- Mahalalel, who lived 895 years, his son was

- Jared, who lived 962 years, his son was

- Enoch, who lived 365 years, his son was

- Methuselah, who lived 969 years, his son was

- Lamech, who lived 777 years, his son was Noah.

As the earth was populated, sin on the earth spread and grew. Most of the world did not know God anymore. The Bible tells us that evil had persisted to the point that God was sorry that He had made man and that "He grieved in His heart."

Noah and his family had been faithful to God, so God told Noah to build an ark. God told Noah to build an ark because He was going to save Noah's family, but destroy the earth with a great flood. Noah had three sons, Shem, Ham, and Japheth, who each had a wife. Along with Noah, his wife, his three sons, and their wives, eight people were saved on the ark. Along with Noah's family, two of every kind of animal were saved on the ark (male and female).

The rain that flooded the earth lasted 40 days and 40 nights. The water prevailed on the earth for 150 days, and it took another 221 days for the waters to recede and the land to be dry enough for Noah, his family, and all the animals to eventually leave the confines of the ark.

Noah and his family worshiped God when they came out of the ark. God put the sign of the rainbow in the sky and made a promise to Noah that He would never destroy the earth again by a flood. The rainbow is the sign of the covenant that God made with Noah. This covenant between God and Noah is called the Noahic Covenant. Now, the earth again had to be repopulated, and it all started this time with Noah and his family.

After the earth became well-populated again, the Bible tells us about an event called the Tower of Babel. All of humankind spoke one language and lived in one place. The Tower of Babel was a tower that man built that would supposedly reach Heaven. It represented mankind's selfishness and idolatry. God realized that this was a problem and scattered man across all the earth, giving them different languages.

Both the great flood in Noah's day and the Tower of Babel are momentous events in Bible history. When thoroughly researched and understood, they help explain many things about how the world came to be today. Also, these events help Christians go deeper in their faith and play an important part in God's salvation plan for man.

Included in the line of Adam and Noah is a man named Abraham. God introduces Himself to Abraham and begins a relationship with him that will raise up a great nation, the Jewish Nation. He journeys with Abraham as he settles in what is modern-day Israel (the land of Canaan at the time). He makes a promise or covenant with Abraham that he will be the father of a great nation. *This covenant between God and Abraham is called the Abrahamic Covenant. From this covenant and nation will come the Messiah and a Savior, Jesus, who will save the world from their sin.* God is in the "covenant-making or promise-making business." He fulfills His purposes on earth by establishing covenants throughout the Bible.

God's promise to Abraham to make him a great nation starts with His promise to provide Abraham with a son. However, Abraham's wife, Sara, has been unable to get pregnant, and as she ages, the two of them begin to doubt God's promise. As a result, and contrary to God's plan, Sara gives her Egyptian maidservant to Abraham to produce this promised son. Sara's maidservant gives birth to a son named Ishmael. As time passes, Sara begins to regret her decision and despises her maidservant and Ishmael. As a result, Abraham sends them away. There is more to the story of Ishmael, however, the promised son for Sara is finally provided, and his name is Isaac, through whom God would fulfill His promise of the Abrahamic covenant.

Before we continue with Isaac's lineage of the Abrahamic promise, you should know an important incident in the life of Isaac that would be a foreshadowing of Jesus' death and resurrection on the cross.

When Isaac was a young man, God told Abraham to take his son (now his only son) and sacrifice him. Why in the world would God do such a thing? Herein lies one of the great mysteries of how God works in the Bible and how many Christians believe God works today.

Because we have the Bible in its entirety and because Christians know the "whole" story of the death and resurrection of Jesus, we can put this request (command) of God in perspective. Additionally, Abraham was a man of tremendous faith, so much so that the Bible tells us that God credited his faith as righteousness. In other words, God gave Abraham credit as being completely righteous because of his faith. This is a powerful concept that the Bible teaches us about who Abraham was and the incredible work that God was doing through the Abrahamic Covenant.

So, Abraham obeys God and takes Isaac to an area of Israel known as Mount Moriah. This is an important location, and many significant things happened there, including the building of the Jewish temple centuries later. As Abraham prepares stones and wood to create an altar for the sacrifice, Isaac asks his father where the traditional lamb or goat is for the sacrifice. As Abraham binds his son upon the altar, raises his arm with a knife in hand to kill Isaac, and then burns him, God speaks to him and stops him from going through with the sacrifice. One of the things that the Bible tells us about this was that it was a test for Abraham. God tells him that He now knows that Abraham is obedient to Him in every way. When they look around, Abraham and Isaac find a ram caught in a thicket, and they sacrifice that ram and worship God together.

What a crazy story, right? It is one of many events in the Bible that has tremendous significance. When you read the Bible and become familiar with these types of events, you will begin to see how they relate and understand their importance. For this event, it is a foreshadowing of God Himself sacrificing His only Son on the cross. However, different from Abraham's situation, God actually gave His Son as a sacrifice and payment for man's sins (our sins—you and me). The power of the resurrection is seen through the faith of Abraham because the Bible teaches that Abraham believed that if he had killed his only son, that God could raise him up again. Now that is FAITH!

Isaac continues to fulfill the Abrahamic promise by having two sons named Esau and Jacob. Isaac blesses Jacob, who has twelve sons who become the twelve tribes of Israel. Three of Jacob's twelve sons become pivotal in bringing about God's promise. Those three sons were named Judah, Levi, and Joseph, who was the youngest son.

Let's start with Joseph. Have you ever heard the story about the "coat of many colors"? This is where that story comes from. The Bible tells us that Joseph was Jacob's favorite son, and the rest of his brothers knew this and were jealous. They hated Joseph, actually. The "coat of many colors" that Joseph wore was an outward sign of this jealousy and hatred. Also, Joseph was a dreamer, and he told his brothers that he had had a dream that one day all of them would bow down to him and serve him.

Because of this, his brothers sold him to slave traders, and he ended up in Egypt, working in Pharaoh's palace, the ruler of Egypt. There is much to glean from Joseph's story, and I am only scratching the surface here. He experienced so many different situations, but in the end, Joseph became a ruler in Egypt, serving right under the authority of Pharaoh.

It just so happened that back in the land of Israel, where Jacob and his sons resided, there was a famine. Jacob sent several of his sons to Egypt to trade for food. When the brothers met Joseph in Egypt's marketplace, they did not recognize Joseph, but Joseph recognized them. Through a series of events, Joseph revealed himself to them, and because of the famine in Israel, he invited Jacob and all his family to live with him in Egypt. When Jacob brought his sons and all their families to Egypt, there were seventy family members in all.

The Jewish nation prospered for many years in Egypt and grew to a nation of millions. However, when the ruling Pharaoh died and the new Pharaoh took over, the Jewish nation became slaves to the Egyptians. They remained in slavery to the Egyptians for over four hundred years until God raised up a leader named Moses to lead them to freedom.

The story of Moses and the freeing of Israel from slavery is found in the second book of the Bible called Exodus. Because the Jewish nation was multiplying so fast, the Egyptian ruler ordered that all male Jewish babies be killed, and the female babies would live. When Moses was born, his mother put him in a basket and sent him down the Nile River to where the Queen of Egypt bathed daily. When the Queen found the child, she raised him as her own. Moses was part of the Egyptian elite and well-educated in the Egyptian schools. He was trained to be a leader.

Moses spent the first forty years of his life in Egypt. As he was performing his duties of supervising the Israelite slaves, he killed an Egyptian guard who was mistreating two Jewish men. As a result of this, Moses fled to the desert, where he lived for the next forty years of his life, herding sheep for his father-in-law.

The "Burning Bush" is another important event in Bible history. It is where God introduces Himself to Moses out of a burning bush. God instructs Moses to return to Egypt and tell Pharaoh to free the Jewish people.

Moses faces great resistance from Pharaoh. Because Pharaoh refuses to give the nation of Israel their freedom, God sends ten plagues on Egypt. The tenth plague is the most devastating and important. God sends the Angel of Death to kill all firstborn males, both Egyptian and Jewish. However, God instructs Moses to tell the Jewish people to sacrifice their best lamb and put its blood on the doorposts and at the top of the door. The Angel of Death would "Passover" the house and not kill any firstborn males inside. *This is another momentous event in Bible history and the history of the*

Jewish nation. This event is called Passover. We will talk about this event again when we discuss the death and resurrection of Jesus.

Pharaoh's firstborn son dies because of this plague. Pharaoh relents and frees the Jewish people. Moses leads the nation of Israel out into the wilderness. At the beginning of their journey, the nation camps at Mt. Sinai, where Moses will receive the Ten Commandments from God. Moses stays with God at the top of Mt. Sinai for forty days before coming down the mountain to give the people these laws. By the time Moses comes down, the people have given up hope and started worshiping the Golden Calf. Essentially, the people turned to idol worship and sinned a great sin against God.

After being in the desert for about two years, the Jewish nation approached the Promised Land of Israel (known as Canaan at the time). God commands them to send out twelve spies to scout the land. When the spies returned, all but two reported that they could not conquer the territory because of the various peoples who currently inhabited it. Because of this, the Bible tells us that the Jewish nation disobeyed God and did not go into the Promised Land. As a result of their disobedience, the Jewish people wandered in the desert for forty years before crossing the Jordan River into the Promised Land. An entire generation would die in the wilderness and never see the land God had promised them.

Moses was a descendant of Levi, Jacob's son, mentioned earlier. The descendants of Levi were called Levites, and they served as priests for the nation of Israel. The priests were responsible for maintaining the temple and performing various ceremonies and sacrifices for the people of Israel.

Led by Moses, the nation of Israel gained their freedom from Egypt and wandered in the wilderness of the Sinai Peninsula for forty years, before making their way to what is now modern-day Israel. Before crossing the Jordan River, Moses was one hundred and twenty years old and died. Joshua, who had been part of the Jewish leadership, became their new leader and led them across the Jordan River into what the Jewish nation had considered God's Promised Land.

This Promised Land territory was divided and ruled by several warring nations. It was considered the land of Canaan, ruled by the Canaanites. However, other nations like the Philistines, Amorites, Hittites, and several others also lived in and controlled parts of the territory. All these nations would fight against Israel to gain control of the land.

As the Jewish nation entered the land known today as Israel, recall that there were twelve Jewish tribes. These twelve tribes were the sons of Jacob (Jacob was the son of Isaac, who was the son of Abraham). The twelve tribes were: Reuben, Simeon, Ephraim,

Judah, Dan, Naphtali, Gad, Asher, Issachar, Zebulun, Manasseh, and Benjamin. (Manasseh and Ephraim were sons of Joseph, and Levi's descendants were priests and did not own territory), While not perfectly executed, the goal of the twelve tribes was to work together to conquer the land and then divide it so that each tribe ruled its own territory.

After Joshua led the Jewish people in the initial conquest of the land, a single leader no longer led the Jewish nation. Instead, Israel was led by a series of Judges in distributed authority roles. The nation of Israel continued to struggle under this leadership structure. Between various battles with the warring nations occupying the land, and the nation's sinful ways in turning against God and worshiping false gods, Israel faced difficulties and eventually called for a King.

Israel's first anointed King was Saul. He was a successful king for a period, and the nation of Israel began to conquer and control a good part of the territory known as Israel. Saul was a good King, but began to drift in his obedience toward God. He made a crucial mistake by blatantly disobeying God regarding one particular battle and took upon himself the role of a priest in making sacrifices to God. As a result, God turned to a young shepherd boy named David from the tribe of Judah to eventually become King and lead the people.

The Bible tells us that David was a "man after God's own heart. Perhaps best known in both Christian and non-Christian circles for having killed Goliath the Philistine with just a stone and a sling, King David was a strong military leader who unified the twelve tribes. He is credited with conquering the land and establishing the occupied nation of Israel.

Besides the famous story of killing Goliath, the Bible tells us many things about King David. While King David was a man of God, he had his own sinful issues, leading to several leadership and personal problems. On one occasion, while his army fought, King David remained at home. From his balcony, he observed a beautiful woman named Bathsheba and summoned her to his palace. Bathsheba was married to Uriah, who was a soldier in King David's army. While Uriah was away fighting, King David had an affair with Bathsheba, and she became pregnant. As a result, David tried to cover it up by sending Uriah to the front lines, where he died in battle. Between adultery and murder, King David directly disobeyed and offended God. Because of David's sin, the child born to David and Bathsheba died. David went on to repent of this horrific sin against God and wrote one of the most poignant passages in the Bible in the book of Psalms (Psalm 51). Bathsheba became David's wife, and they would go on to have another son through whom God would continue to deliver His promises. David's son, who would succeed him as King of Israel, was named Solomon.

Before I continue with the story of Solomon, it's important to mention something here regarding David's behavior and sin. If you ever start reading and studying the Bible, you will realize that it is full of flawed men and women just like you and me. *God uses flawed people, and despite their sinfulness, God accomplishes His plan.* It is an amazing thing to see repeatedly throughout the Bible. Keep in mind, God's plan at this point is to create the nation of Israel, which would bring about a Messiah named Jesus. David is a descendant from the tribe of Judah, and Judah is the son of Jacob, the son of Isaac, the son of Abraham. God continued to fulfill the Abrahamic Covenant through David and his son Solomon.

King Solomon is considered the wisest and wealthiest of all the Kings of Israel. At an early age, God told Solomon he could ask for anything he wanted, and God would grant it to him. Solomon prayed and asked for wisdom. *The incredible and vast wisdom of Solomon created the most unified and peaceful period the nation of Israel has ever known.*

Besides his wealth and fame at the time, King Solomon is best known for building the Jewish temple in Jerusalem. God had denied David the opportunity to build the temple because King David was a warring ruler. However, during his lifetime, King David collected most of the supplies used by his son Solomon to build the temple.

King Solomon lived much of his life obeying and leading the Jewish people faithfully. However, as mentioned above, with God using flawed men, towards the end of his life, Solomon strayed, marrying foreign women and introducing pagan and foreign gods into the Jewish lifestyle. Eventually, after King Solomon's death, this would lead the nation of Israel on a continuous path of turning away from their one true God and then constantly turning back to Him.

After Solomon's time, God raised up both good and bad kings of Israel. The nation soon splintered and divided into a northern and southern kingdom. Because of this division and their sinfulness, the Jewish people were eventually conquered by Persia, leading to exile in Babylon for seventy years.

God raised up various prophets (considered major and minor prophets, see the division of books in the list of the Old Testament at the back) to eventually call the nation of Israel back to God and Jerusalem, where the temple would be rebuilt. After the last book of the Old Testament, Malachi, God is silent regarding the nation of Israel for four hundred years. We do not have any account or history for this four-hundred-year period, and as the Bible picks up in the New Testament, we find that the nation of Israel is now occupied by the Romans. Rome has conquered the land of Israel, and the Jewish people are living in their own land as a conquered nation.

Recall the SIN problem I mentioned earlier, when Israel was wandering in the wilderness for forty years under Moses' leadership? God established various sacrifices to address this SIN problem. These sacrifices served as a way for the people to be forgiven for their sins. The sacrifices involved distinct types of animals, depending on which sacrifice they were making. It was the priests from the tribe of Levi who were responsible for overseeing God's sacrificial system.

The sacrificial system for forgiving sin is important to understand because God demanded payment through a blood sacrifice (death). Various types of animals were killed and offered as payment. This was a way for Israel to pay for their sins and maintain a relationship with God. But there was a big problem with this system, it was temporary! The people would have to continue to come back to the priest repeatedly as they committed various sins. The main sacrifice, called the Day of Atonement, was intended to cover all sin for the people, and it was performed once a year. However, this sacrifice was only once a year, and it occurred on the same day, year after year. Again, it was a temporary solution.

So, how would God resolve the temporary nature of forgiving sins? This is where Jacob's son Judah plays a key role. God promised the nation of Israel an ultimate King who would rule the nation and provide the ultimate sacrifice for the forgiveness of sins. He was called the Messiah. *Messiah means a promised deliverer, leader, and*

Savior.[4] The Messiah would be a descendant of Jacob's son Judah, and His name would be Jesus.

Who is Jesus and what was His purpose? In the following chapter, "What about this Jesus," I want to spend time telling you about who Jesus was/is and His ministry on earth. In the chapter after that, when we discuss the Good News, we will address Jesus' purpose and what that means for everyone. Getting to know Jesus is a lifelong journey for the Christian. Understanding what He did and what He offers the world (the Good News) is the most important thing people can know.

---

[4]"Messiah," *Dictionary.com*, accessed September 8, 2025, https://www.dictionary.com/browse/messiah.

Chapter 5

What about this Jesus?

In the previous chapter, entitled "Basics Before the Basics," I talked about the concept of God being in the form of The Trinity, God the Father, God the Son (Jesus), and God the Holy Spirit. In this chapter, I would like to focus on who Jesus is as part of this "3 in 1" Godhead. Again, the concept of the Trinity is a topic all by itself, and scholars are still writing in-depth discussions of exactly what that means. So, the first important thing to know about Jesus is that **He is the Son of God.**

Besides being God's Son, what else is there about Jesus? What does He mean to the Christian faith?

First, it is important to understand that Jesus has existed for all eternity, just like God the Father and God the Holy Spirit. In the Bible, in the book of John, John, the author of this book, writes that Jesus was in the beginning (the beginning of time as we know it) and was with God (God the Father), and that Jesus is actually God (John 1:1). **Jesus is Eternal, He is God.**

Recall what I said about Jesus being a part of the creation process? Well, this is important because John continues and tells us that *all things were made through Jesus*. In other words, He plays a part and is responsible for bringing about creation in the first place. This emphasis on Jesus (God the Son) being with God the Father for all eternity and being a part of the creation story is the beginning of understanding the next role that Jesus plays. **Jesus is the Creator.**

From our conversation back in Chapter 4, we know that a problem between God and man existed called SIN. SIN separates us from God, and we cannot have a relationship with God if our SIN exists between us. God cannot and will not remain in the presence of SIN, and therefore, if man lives in his SIN, there can be no relationship.

So how do "we" (man) solve this problem? Since the beginning of time, man has attempted to solve the SIN problem in more ways than we can imagine. The main way that man tries to solve the SIN problem is to make himself/herself their own God. What do I mean by this?

Well, it is as simple as taking God out of the equation and saying that He simply does not exist. Another way to say this is that people simply "dismiss" God. If you are one of those people, then hopefully it's one of the reasons that you are reading this book, to learn more about why you believe what you believe and/or why you don't believe what you don't believe. If a person says that God does not exist, then they would conclude, "I don't have a SIN problem."

When man tries to make himself his own God, he thinks he is in control. As man, he feels like he can direct things as necessary, bringing about the desired outcome. We see this happening all around our world today in so many ways.

Taking away the fact that there was a creator of the universe and replacing it with a theory of evolution is another way of explaining away the existence of God. How about Global Warming? Have you ever thought that Global Warming is a way to dismiss the existence of God? Does man really have any control of the environment (I am speaking on an exceptionally large scale here)? If man really had control over the earth's climate, wouldn't that alleviate the need for a God? While man can do some common-sense things to be a responsible steward of the world around us, there are only certain levels in which he participates.

The Bible teaches that God *holds the universe together*. He is active on the Earth and controls everything to keep it in balance and man alive. The rotation of the earth, the distance from the sun, the moon, and its effect on the tides, and the seasons are all held together by God in every moment of every day. Have you ever considered that God is the one who keeps the universe intact? Can man really control the warming or cooling of the earth? Can we even measure that? Jesus, as Creator, is directly involved.

So, back to Jesus and this SIN problem. As we discussed previously regarding God establishing the Jewish people and the nation of Israel in the book of Genesis, God initially provided a way to solve the SIN problem through priests who would make sacrifices of several types of animals for the people. There were all kinds of sacrifices throughout the year to resolve all types of different SINS. In addition, recall the annual sacrifice called the Day of Atonement. The Day of Atonement was meant to remind the people of their sinfulness and need for forgiveness. The priest would enter the center of the temple, called the Holy of Holies, to ask forgiveness on behalf of all the people.

There was still another problem with this process once completed each year. Each year, the people, through various sacrifices and the priest who would intercede, had to return the following year and repeat the same ritual. The fact that the priest had to repeat this ceremonial sacrifice every year demonstrates its temporariness. The SIN problem did not go away permanently, and it was not resolved permanently.

What man could not do for himself, God took it upon Himself to solve the problem and offer a way to take away people's SIN. *Jesus was the answer to the SIN problem, and as God's Son, He came to be the ultimate sacrifice for man's SIN.* Since God is a God of justice, a payment was due to resolve man's SIN of disobedience. Jesus came to earth to pay the SIN debt that we could not pay. He was sent in the form of man, just like us, and He lived a perfect life until He died like us. Unlike us, after being buried in a tomb for three days, He rose from the dead. Christians believe and the Bible teaches that Jesus "conquered" death.

The Bible tells us that Jesus experienced all the same things in life that you and I have experienced or will experience. There is nothing that Jesus cannot understand about the circumstances of your life. This is just a part of what makes Him so special. **Jesus is the Savior of the world.**

How did Jesus come to earth if He was in Heaven with God the Father? Have you heard the term "Virgin Birth?" The virgin birth of Jesus is one of the most central beliefs of the Christian faith. Jesus had an earthly mother, and her name was Mary. However, Jesus was not conceived by an earthly father—enter the third part of the Trinity, the Holy Spirit. Jesus was conceived by the Holy Spirit with Mary, who was a virgin. Jesus was born out of a Virgin Birth.

If you have had little to no exposure to Christianity, I am guessing this is going to make no sense, or you think it simply sounds like nonsense. Well, believe me, I can understand completely.

It took me most of my life to get comfortable with how that could have worked. It took extensive reading, research, and yes, faith.

As a result of this union, when Jesus was born, He was both fully God and fully Man, another central belief of the Christian faith. This is important because the man part of God is the one who lived a life that we could not live. He lived a perfect life. A life that was WITHOUT SIN. This life without SIN is part of what qualifies Jesus to resolve the SIN problem between man and God. Also, it is important and comforting to Christians to consider that because Jesus was fully man, He lived a life like we do. He lived as a human and understood our humanity. The Bible teaches that there is nothing that we experience that Jesus did not experience. This is particularly comforting to Christians when they are going through a difficult experience. Christians consider this as they are going through all walks of life, whether good or bad.

Jesus was fully God and fully Man.

In the Old Testament, the Bible tells us that the nation of Israel (Jews) anticipated a coming King who would lead the nation of Israel and rule all the kingdoms of the earth. To the Jewish nation, this King was their Messiah (deliverer and Savior)[5] because He would save them from all their enemies. **Jesus is the Messiah.**

---

[5]"Messiah," *Dictionary.com*, accessed September 8, 2025, https://www.dictionary.com/browse/messiah.

Have you ever heard the phrase "born to die?" Jesus was truly a man that was born to die. As you have read previously, Jesus' entire purpose was to suffer and die on a cross for the sins of the world so that you and I could be "reconciled" to God and have a relationship with Him. You will often hear Christians use the word "redeemed." The Bible teaches that if a person believes and receives Jesus as their Lord and Savior, then they are "redeemed" and "reconciled" to God.

While it was Jesus' purpose to save all humanity, what about His life on earth? How did He go about spending His time, and what was His journey like? How did He live, and how did He accomplish His intended purpose?

At the time of Jesus' birth, the Romans occupied the nation of Israel. Roman governors were assigned territories in various regions of Israel. King Herod of Rome was assigned the region where Jesus was born. Jesus was born in Bethlehem, which is a town in Israel just south of Jerusalem. His mother was Mary, and his earthly father was Joseph.

Up to and through the time of Jesus' birth, King Herod had heard about the birth of a coming Jewish Messiah that would lead the nation of Israel. So, because he considered this a threat to him and the Roman government, he ordered that all first-born males between a specific time be put to death.

Because of this, Mary and Joseph fled to Egypt until King Herod died, and the threat passed (about two years). When they returned from Egypt, Mary, Joseph, and Jesus settled in Nazareth (a town about forty miles north of Jerusalem) where Jesus grew up.

So, Jesus was born in Bethlehem and as an infant, fled to Egypt, where He stayed until He was two years old. The Bible does not give an account of Jesus next until He is twelve years old. As this young boy of twelve, we get a glimpse of His awareness of who He was and what His ministry was about. The Bible tells us that Jesus traveled with His parents and a large group of people in their community to a distant town and marketplace to buy various goods. When the caravan loaded up and left on the return journey, unbeknownst to His parents, Jesus stayed behind. By the time Mary and Joseph discovered Jesus was missing and returned to find Him, they found Jesus in the Jewish temple (synagogue), listening to the Jewish priests who were instructing the people. Jesus was even participating in the teaching, and when His parents saw and heard this, they were astonished.

Christians understand from this story that Jesus had insight into who He was and what His ministry was to be, even at this youthful age. When Mary and Joseph confronted Jesus in the temple, *Jesus responded by saying, "Why did you seek Me? Did you not know that I must be about My Father's business?"* (Luke 2:49

NKJV). The Bible's account of Jesus' self-awareness as a youth is simply fascinating. This is the only account of Jesus as a youth.

The next time the Bible mentions Jesus is when He begins His three-year ministry around the age of thirty. Jesus' ministry begins when John the Baptist (Jesus' cousin) baptizes Him. John the Baptist was a prophet. His role was to prepare the way for Jesus' ministry. He preached a message of repentance and told the Jewish nation that the Kingdom of God was at hand. It is the first time that we hear about baptism in the Bible, and it is important that John baptizes Jesus, not that He needed to be cleansed of any SINS, but it served as an example for the people and serves as an example for Christians today. *Baptism is the outward sign of the Christian faith.* It is an important act of obedience to publicly express one's commitment to follow Jesus. Also, Jesus is publicly expressing His commitment and obedience to God the Father. Jesus' baptism was substitutional, much like His crucifixion on the cross. His righteousness has now become our righteousness.

The Bible tells us that the Holy Spirit draws Jesus out to the desert wilderness, where He stays for forty days and forty nights fasting and praying. (For now, just know that fasting is the practice of denying oneself food and/or water for a period.)

Jesus is preparing for His three-year ministry and His journey to His crucifixion. While He is in the desert wilderness, Satan tempts Him. The Bible tells us that Satan tempted Jesus three times. Satan's first temptation was concerning food. Satan asks Jesus if He is really the Son of God, to turn stone into bread. Jesus answers by quoting an Old Testament passage concerning that man does not live on bread alone. Satan asks a second time that if Jesus is truly the Son of God, to throw Himself off the mountaintop and let the angels save Him. Jesus replies again with an Old Testament passage of not tempting the Lord. Finally, Satan shows Jesus all the kingdoms of the earth and says he will give them to Jesus if He just bows down and worships him. Again, Jesus quotes an Old Testament passage about not tempting the Lord your God and sends Satan away. The next time that Jesus will encounter Satan personally like this is in Jerusalem in the Garden of Gethsemane, just before Jesus is arrested to be crucified.

When Jesus returns from His time in the desert wilderness, He then begins His ministry by calling His twelve disciples. When I say "calls," Jesus would ask each disciple to "follow Me." The words "follow Me" are extremely important to Christians who pursue a relationship with Jesus Christ. We will discuss them in the next chapter entitled "Good News for the World."

Jesus had twelve disciples. The twelve disciples were Peter, Andrew, James, John, Matthew, Thomas, Simon, Philip, Bartholomew, Thaddaeus, James, and Judas. These men were considered common and not educated. Most of these men were fishermen. Matthew was a tax collector. While common and not necessarily considered educated, these men had heard about the coming Messiah and were looking for Him. When they initially met Jesus, something was different to them. Some of them recognized Jesus as the Messiah right away, and others considered it readily enough that they began to follow Him and learn from Him. As they grew to know Jesus and trust Him, all became His disciples and participated with Him in His three-year ministry. Apart from Judas, all the disciples accepted Jesus as the chosen Messiah and worked to spread the Good News.

As mentioned previously, *Jesus' entire ministry is recounted in the first four books of the New Testament called the Gospels (the books of Matthew, Mark, Luke, and John).* Here is a summary of what we have discussed so far about Jesus' ministry.

- The genealogy from Adam to Jesus is documented in the Gospels.

- John the Baptist is born (Jesus' cousin).

- Jesus is conceived and born of the Holy Spirit and Virgin Mary.

- Jesus, Mary, and Joseph fled to Egypt for two years.

- Jesus, Mary, and Joseph return to Israel and settle in Nazareth.

- Jesus learns and teaches in the temple at age twelve.

- John the Baptist baptizes Jesus.

- Jesus' ministry begins around age 30.

- Jesus calls His twelve disciples to, "Follow Me."

For the next three years, Jesus and His disciples traveled around the country of Israel teaching the Jewish nation and performing countless miracles. Jesus was preparing the Jewish nation for a New Covenant with God. Previously, they had been under the Abrahamic (and Mosaic) Covenants, which were based on the Law, specifically the Ten Commandments. Now, Jesus was preparing them for the new Covenant of Grace. This new covenant would be a promise of eternal life through His death and resurrection on the cross. It would be a promise of hope and forgiveness based on Jesus' gift of salvation, which Christians consider free.

One of the ways Jesus taught was through parables. (A parable is a short story that teaches a moral principle or spiritual concept, not readily revealed, necessarily.) The subjects of Jesus' parables were wide-ranging, but typically appropriate for the intended audience. For example, there were parables that He shared with everyday crowds, but then there were parables that Jesus shared specifically for the Jewish leadership of the day (the Sadducees and Pharisees).

The reason for teaching in parables is best explained by Jesus himself in the book of Matthew, chapter 13, verses 10-17.

The Purpose of the Parables

> [10] And the disciples came and said to Him, "Why do You speak to them in parables?" [11] He answered and said to them, "Because it has been given to you to know the mysteries of the kingdom of Heaven, but to them it has not been given. [12] For whoever has, to him more will be given, and he will have abundance; but whoever does not have, even what he has will be taken away from him. [13] Therefore I speak to them in parables, because seeing they do not see, and hearing they do not hear, nor do they understand. [14] And in them the prophecy of Isaiah is fulfilled, which says:
> 'Hearing you will hear and shall not understand,
> And seeing you will see and not perceive;
>
> [15] For the hearts of this people have grown dull.
> *Their* ears are hard of hearing,
> And their eyes they have closed,
> Lest they should see with their eyes and hear with their ears,
> Lest they should understand with their hearts and turn,
> So that I should heal them.'
> [16] But blessed are your eyes for they see, and your ears for they hear; [17] for assuredly, I say to you that many prophets and righteous men desired to see what you see, and did not see it, and to hear what you hear, and did not hear it.

Jesus was telling His disciples that the parables were for them so that they could learn more about Him and His Kingdom. Jesus was telling His disciples that they were blessed because God the Father had revealed the meanings of parables to them. He was saying that if the people would turn from their old ways and open their hearts, Jesus would heal them. The Jewish leaders would never understand what Jesus meant when He taught in parables, because their hearts were hard. They refused to consider what Jesus was offering them because He threatened the status quo and the leader's position among the Jewish people.

Jesus developed relationships, instructed the people, and performed many miracles. The Jewish people called Him a teacher. The miracles included healing people, miracles of nature, resurrection miracles, and other supernatural events.

One of Jesus' more notable relationship encounters was with "the woman at the well." We do not know her name, but do know that she was a Samaritan woman. Jesus had chosen to travel through the region known as Samaria, even though it was not the customary route from Galilee (northern Israel) to Jerusalem, and the southern region of Israel.

After Jesus sends His disciples into the town of Samaria for food, He meets this Samaritan woman at a well where she is drawing water in the middle of the day. She was there during that time because she knew no one else would be there. This Samaritan woman had a reputation among the people in the town, and Jesus was about to tell her all about her life. When Jesus asks her for a drink of water, the woman quickly recognizes that Jesus is Jewish.

She is Samaritan, and traditionally, Samaritans and Jews did not interact and hated one another.

She says she is not married, but Jesus tells her that indeed that is true because the man she is living with now is not her husband. Previously, she had five other men who were not her husband. The Samaritan woman marvels at the fact that Jesus knows all about her.

Jesus uses the water in the well as a metaphor for Himself. He talks about those who drink water from the well will thirst again, but those who drink from the living water which Jesus offers will never thirst again. The woman tells Jesus that she wants this living water and asks, where can she get some?

Jesus goes on to tell her that He is the Messiah, the one even the Samaritans were looking for. After they finish their conversation, the woman is so excited that she rushes back into town and tells everyone they must come out to meet the man who knew everything about her. Jesus and the disciples stay in Samaria for several days, preaching and teaching. Even after they leave, the woman at the well continues to tell others about Jesus and that He is the coming Messiah and Savior that they have been seeking.

One of my favorite healing miracles is recounted in the book of John, chapter 9, when Jesus restores a blind man's sight. One of the reasons it is a favorite is that it reads like a soap opera. It has several unique characters, and the story takes several twists and turns. The story has multiple in-depth spiritual lessons as well.

Jesus and His disciples are walking along when they come across a blind man sitting on the side of the road. The disciples ask Jesus who had sinned in life in order that this man was born blind. They asked, was it the blind man or his parents specifically? You see, Jewish custom and belief taught that if you were unfortunate, poor, disabled, or had any misfortune in your life, that God was punishing the person for their sins. This could be the person themselves or one of their family members.

Jesus' answer to His disciples was that neither the blind man nor his parents had sinned. Jesus says that *this man had been born blind so that the works of God could be displayed through this man's life.*

Jesus bends down in front of the blind man, spits in the dirt, and puts a hand of mud patches on each eye. He tells the blind man to go wash it off in a healing pool of water. The blind man does, and his sight, absent since birth, was restored. The people in the community were astonished, and some did not believe that he had been blind since birth. They took the blind man to see the Jewish leaders, who questioned him repeatedly.

The blind man told the Jewish leaders that a man named Jesus had healed him. They questioned the blind man about his relationship with Jesus, but as the blind man explained, he did not know anything about Jesus. He explained that he did not know Jesus at all. The Jewish leaders even called the blind man's parents in and questioned them. The blind man's parents did not want to get in trouble with the Jewish leaders, so their response was that their son was of age and old enough to speak for himself.

The blind man stood up for himself in front of the Jewish leadership. He reasoned with them that restoring a blind person's sight was a good thing, and since it was a good thing, it had to be the work of God. The Jewish leadership argued that this could not be since Jesus was a sinner. The blind man responded by saying if Jesus were a sinner, and not from God, that He could do nothing. The blind man was using the Jewish belief system of the day to rebut their argument. In the end, the Jewish leadership threw the blind man out of the temple. In today's terminology, they excommunicated him from the Jewish church.

The story ends beautifully. When Jesus heard that the blind man had been thrown out of the temple, He sought out and found the blind man. Jesus asked the once-blind man if he believed in the Son of God. When the once-blind man asked who the Son of God was, *Jesus told him that He was Jesus, the Son of God.* The once-blind man now knew who Jesus was and believed in Him.

Jesus had power over life and death. He resurrected people who had died. One of my favorite resurrection miracles of Jesus was when He raised His friend Lazarus from the dead. The story is recounted in the book of John, chapter 11.

Jesus and His disciples were traveling when they got word that Jesus' friend Lazarus was seriously ill. Jesus did not go to Lazarus immediately but remained two days where He was before arriving at Lazarus' home. When Jesus arrived, Lazarus was already dead and buried. Lazarus' sisters, Mary (different from the mother of Jesus) and Martha, were in mourning. They pleaded with Jesus that if He had only come sooner, Lazarus would still be alive.

The shortest passage in the Bible is found here. In the book of John, chapter 11, verse 35, it reads, "Jesus wept." This passage tells us so much about the humanness of Jesus. Obviously, He had a strong relationship with these siblings and considered them a part of His family. It demonstrates His compassion and love.

So, Jesus instructed that the stone be removed from the tomb. Lazarus' body had been prepared, as was Jewish custom, and his body was wrapped in bandages. Jesus told Lazarus to come forth and come out of the tomb. As Lazarus made his way out of the tomb, still wrapped in bandages, the people who saw this were amazed. Many who witnessed this event believed in Jesus, but others went away, not believing, and even went to the Jewish leadership to report what had happened.

Jesus had power over nature as well. One of the best-known instances of this among Christians is when Jesus calmed a storm as He and His disciples were crossing the Sea of Galilee, a region of Israel. In another demonstration of His power over nature, Jesus walked on water.

Jesus worked with His disciples over the course of a three-year ministry. His goal was to teach the Jewish nation who He was and what He was offering them. Their previous way of life was based on the promises that God had made through Abraham in what the Bible calls the Abrahamic Covenant, as mentioned in the previous chapter entitled "It Starts with the First Book."

As a quick review to put Jesus' coming in perspective, the first book of the Bible, Genesis, recounts that Abraham had a son named Isaac. Isaac had a son named Jacob. God changed the name of Jacob to Israel, and God's Abrahamic covenant continued through Jacob's sons, known as the twelve tribes of Israel (Reuben, Simeon, Ephraim, Judah, Dan, Naphtali, Gad, Asher, Issachar, Zebulun, Manasseh, and Benjamin). As mentioned previously, Joseph's descendants helped build the nation of Israel (Manasseh and Ephraim were sons of Joseph), Levi's descendants helped lead the nation of Israel as priests, and Judah's descendants would provide the promised Messiah and Savior, named Jesus. Jesus would offer the New Covenant of Salvation through His death and resurrection on the cross.

As Jesus was ending His three-year ministry, He journeyed to Jerusalem to fulfill His purpose, as He would be executed and crucified by the Jews and the Romans. As He arrived in Jerusalem, celebrations had begun for what was known as the Passover. If you recall, this is an annual celebration to remember the nation of Israel's release from captivity and slavery in Egypt (from the book of Genesis in the Bible). In our current day and time, the day of Jesus' triumphant entry into Jerusalem is known as Palm Sunday. The entire week leading up to Passover is now commonly known as Easter and is called Holy Week.

In the days leading up to Jesus' arrest, He confronts the leaders of the Jewish nation (the Pharisees and Sadducees). Several noteworthy events happened.

One, Jesus went to the Jewish temple right in the heart of Jerusalem and disrupted the commerce that was taking place in the outer parts of the temple. He overturned the trading tables and scattered the merchants' goods and money. This was an incredible display of Jesus establishing His authority. Jesus famously told the crowd that His Father's house (God the Father) would not be turned into a "den of thieves."

In another confrontation with the Jewish leadership, Jesus told them that He would tear down the temple and raise it up again in three days. This was a reference to His own death and resurrection that would take place later that week.

In addition to His confrontation with the Jewish leadership, Jesus had some poignant time and conversations with His disciples. On one occasion, Jesus was with His disciples on the hillside looking over the city of Jerusalem (the hillside is called the Mt. of Olives). Jesus told His disciples of His coming death and resurrection, as well as events that would happen in the future. Some of these future events would happen during the disciples' lifetime, and others are yet to happen to this day. The Bible's account of these conversations coincides and is evidenced by other scripture in the Bible. These various depictions of future events are known today as the "End Times."

Besides Jesus' arrest, the most important event leading up to Jesus' crucifixion is known as the "Last Supper." *The "Last Supper" is what Christians celebrate today as "Holy Communion."* As Jesus was preparing to be arrested and crucified, He sat down with His disciples for a final meal consisting of bread and wine (fermented or non-fermented wine is a constant debate in the Christian community). The bread and wine represented Jesus' body and blood, and His sacrifice on the Cross. Jesus told His disciples that the meal represented the New Covenant, which He was establishing by being the perfect and final sacrifice to redeem humankind from their sins. The New Covenant is one that offers Grace to the world and is the only way for man to be permanently cleansed from sin and come back into a relationship with God. Not only would man on earth now have a relationship with God if they received this free gift, but they would go to Heaven to live with God forever.

After the Last Supper, Jesus was betrayed by Judas, one of His disciples. Jesus was arrested by Roman guards and brought to trial before the Jewish leadership. Jesus appeared before both the Jewish and Roman leadership on two occasions. Jesus' arrest and trial were extremely political. The Jewish leaders had decided that they wanted Jesus crucified for many varied reasons, but essentially, He posed a threat to Jewish beliefs and customs. However, because Rome occupied and ruled Israel, the Jewish leaders were dependent upon Roman leadership to help conduct such a sentencing. Besides being detained, the Romans had Jesus beaten and tortured. Because it was during the Passover celebration (a holiday), it was customary to release a prisoner. The Jewish leaders enticed the crowd to have another criminal released other than Jesus. Again, politics played a role. Finally, Jesus was sentenced to die by the Roman-style execution of crucifixion on a cross.

The timing of this was important. According to Jewish law, He could not be crucified on the Jewish Sabbath, which ran from Friday night at sundown to Saturday night at sundown. The crucifixion process was excruciating. Jesus had to carry His own cross to His own execution. He was outstretched on a wooden cross with each hand nailed, while His feet were nailed together toward the bottom of the cross. The Roman guards raised the cross upright, and Jesus hung there and died within a three-hour period.

Jesus was not crucified alone. Jesus was crucified between two other criminals called "thieves," one on His right and one on His left. The Bible recounts a conversation between these two thieves. One of the thieves mocked Jesus and said that if He really was a King and God, He should save Himself and save them. The other thief defended Jesus, saying that Jesus had done nothing wrong. This thief then asked Jesus to remember him when Jesus established His Kingdom. Jesus replied to this thief and told him that today he would be with Jesus in Paradise. This is one of seven things that Jesus said during those three hours on the cross. The seven things that Jesus said are listed here:

1. Father, forgive them, they don't know what they're doing.

2. Today you will be with Me in paradise (to the thief on the cross).

3. My God, my God, why have you forsaken Me?

4. Woman, behold your son; behold your mother (to Mary and John).

5. I am thirsty.

6. It is finished.

7. Father, I commit my Spirit into Your hands.

Jesus died on what today is known as Good Friday and was buried. Essentially, Christians consider Him to have been crucified on the Passover (Jewish celebration). This is significant because the celebration of Passover marked the day that the nation of Israel gained their freedom from Egyptian slavery.

Jesus had been dead for three days, after which He appeared resurrected to those first witnesses. He appeared to the disciples many separate times and even appeared to more than five hundred people at the same time. Jesus told His disciples that it was to their advantage that He go away because God the Father would send the Holy Spirit, who would help them and the world. He instructed the disciples to go back to Jerusalem and wait for ten days for the Holy Spirit to come. Jesus was on earth for forty days after His resurrection before ascending back to Heaven. Today, Christians celebrate Pentecost as the day the Holy Spirit came to be with the disciples and in the world. The Holy Spirit would empower and lead the disciples to share the Good News about Jesus and start the church. *Jesus' death, burial, and resurrection for the forgiveness of sin in the world is called the Good News (the Gospel).* Let's talk more about The Good News for the World!

Chapter 6

The Good News for the World

Would you believe that the main purpose of the Bible is to share one main message with everyone in the world? Have you heard about what the Bible calls the Good News? Does the world want Good News? How about the "GREATEST NEWS?"

When you hear Christians talk about the Good News, you will hear them refer to it as *"The Gospel."* Gospel is a Greek word which means "Good News." And because this Good News is about Jesus, you will often hear Christians say that it is the "Good News of Jesus Christ."

This Good News is a gift of God. It is free. Many Christians get confused and think you must do something to earn this gift. They spend all their lives jumping through "hoops" to earn God's favor so that they can consider themselves deserving or worthy to go to Heaven. While it does not cost you and me anything for this gift, it cost God the life of His Son, Jesus. It cost Jesus everything!

Because the following is one of the most important Bible verses ever written, I want to quote this one from the book of John in the New Testament. It sums up the Good News in one Bible passage and is one of the most quoted Bible passages.

"FOR GOD SO LOVED THE WORLD THAT HE GAVE HIS ONLY BEGOTTEN SON, THAT WHOEVER BELIEVES IN HIM SHOULD NOT PERISH BUT HAVE EVERLASTING LIFE." (JOHN CHAPTER 3, VERSE 16)

This is the Good News (the Gospel) in its simplest form. However, what is the Good News explained in the most straightforward way?

- All men are sinners and fall short of God's standard.

- The consequence of SIN is death and eternal Hell.

- Payment was required because of Man's sin.

- Jesus came to Earth and lived a SINLESS life.

- Jesus died on a cross as a perfect sacrifice.

- Jesus was buried for 3 days.

- On the 3rd day, Jesus rose from the dead and lives today.

- If a person confesses that they are a sinner and believes that Jesus died for their sin, they will live in Heaven with God and other believers FOREVER.

The Cross and Crucifixion of Jesus Christ is the focal point of the Bible and Christianity. At the cross when Jesus died, four things came together at the same time and changed all eternity.

Sin

When Adam and Eve disobeyed God in the Garden of Eden, as written in the book of Genesis, Sin entered man and all of creation. This Sin was disobedience towards God's instructions and design, and man was separated spiritually from God. This sin goes beyond merely a one-time disobedience for people; it opened a spiritual sinfulness that is the nature of every child born. The Bible teaches that when we are born, we are born into sin. Our very nature is sin.

I have heard both believers and non-believers alike talk about the fact that there are good people in the world. I have sat with a close non-believing friend of mine and shared with him that there will be so-called "good people" that will not be in Heaven. He shared with me that he wanted no part of a God like that.

Do you feel the same way? When you hear that there are some "good people" who will not be in Heaven, how does that make you feel? Do you think that is narrow-minded?

Understanding your own fallibility and sinfulness is the beginning of understanding the need for a God who can help you and save you. We are all human, and humans make mistakes. Whether you know the laws of God and the morality of God that the Bible teaches, most people agree that there is a "basic" right and wrong. Understanding the difference between making a simple, sinless mistake versus committing a sinful mistake provides insight into a deeper understanding of our vulnerability as humans.

Another concept the Bible teaches about sin is in relation to the Ten Commandments. The Ten Commandments stand as God's given guidelines, which encompass all types of sin. The Ten Commandments are often referred to as "The Law." The Bible teaches that if you have broken one law, you have broken all of them. This concept helps us understand how vulnerable and fallible we really are. It helps Christians learn that "sin is sin." While humankind may look at various sins and want to rank some sins as worse than others, all sin is equal in that it is sin. And while the consequences of different sins are not equal, nevertheless, sin is sin, and all of mankind falls short of a perfect and Holy God.

Jesus came to live the perfect sinless life that we could not. The Bible teaches that Jesus is both fully God and fully man. As a man on earth, Jesus experienced everything that you and I have faced or will face in our lives. Because Jesus lived His entire life without sin, He qualifies to be the perfect sacrifice for our sins. God required a perfect sacrifice. God would not accept just any man to die on a cross, because you see, any man would be a sinner. Only Jesus, the Son of God, could live that perfect life.

Judgment

God required judgment for sin, and because of this, there was payment due. God is the judge. There is no one higher. As a judge, He is a God of Justice. He is the ultimate Judge, and man's sin required an accounting. If God did not require a payment for man's sin, He would not be Just. He would not be true to Himself. Being a Just God is part of His nature.

It is no different than when we break human law today. If we run a stop sign and get caught, the payment will be a financial one in the form of a fine. If we steal something from the store and get caught, we may pay a fine and must do community service. If we harm someone severely or commit murder, the payment results in serving time in prison. We have a justice system, and it is there to provide judgment when people commit crimes. In any case, there are consequences to our actions, and a payment of some sort is required.

God required a payment for man's sin. This payment had to be in the form of shedding blood and death. The only one who could do this was God's son, Jesus. In the book of Romans, chapter 3, verse 26, it says that God is both just and the justifier. In other words, He sits as judge, but Jesus, being God, was the justifier (the one who provided payment). God both required the payment and gave the payment.

Jesus is man's substitute. He is our substitute. Instead of God killing Adam and Eve for their sin, He made another way for man to get back to God and have a perfect relationship with Him. Instead of it being a sinful man or an animal with flaws, God provided the perfect substitute in Jesus. Substitute is an important concept. The Bible uses the word *propitiation*. The word *propitiation* means "substitute," and Jesus was that substitute. That is the reason that if we believe in Him as our substitute and Savior, then spiritually His righteousness becomes our righteousness, and God sees us as having never sinned before. According to the book of John, chapter 19, verse 30, when Jesus hung on the cross, the last thing that He said was, *"It is finished."*

When Jesus said these words, He meant it. He meant that by His blood and death, and then His resurrection after 3 days, that all of humankind could have a way back to God. Jesus' act on the cross, His burial, and resurrection served as God's payment for man's sin. God's nature and requirement for justice were fulfilled. God's wrath toward sin was fulfilled. Justice was satisfied.

Forgiveness & Grace

While sin and justice came together on the cross, forgiveness was there too. God was willing to forgive anyone who would receive the sacrifice of Jesus as sin and judgment.

Grace is unmerited favor. Grace is something that we do not deserve. Because God is a God of Grace, He first sought us. God has pursued man throughout all history repeatedly, even when man has rejected Him. He offers Grace, which is His unmerited favor and forgiveness. It was made possible because of what Jesus did on the cross.

Previously, we talked about free will and that God gives man a choice. He does not force anyone to believe what you have read in this book or the Bible. He does not require that you even believe what other Christians say. You are free to choose. For those who would come to believe in Jesus, He offers forgiveness from their sin, and as mentioned, He offers the righteousness of Jesus Christ as a substitute for man's unrighteousness.

Love

Finally, *God's Love is demonstrated at the Cross* as well. Is this weird for you to hear, much less believe?

When I have shared with non-believers that the Bible teaches that there is only one way to Heaven, they find that hard to believe, and most are very much offended. They ask, if God loves people so much, why would He provide only one way to get to Heaven? What about all the other religions in the world? Aren't there many ways to get to Heaven?

The Bible teaches, and true Christians believe, that God loved man and the world so much that He provided this one way. Christians who really understand this pray to God and thank Him that there is even "ONE" way. Consider, did God really have to provide a way at all? Did He really have to provide even just one way? The Bible teaches that God is God. He is in charge, and He can do whatever He pleases. Recall when I introduced the concept of the Trinity. As God the Father, God the Son, and God the Holy Spirit, He is complete. Even though He really does not need us, out of His love, He created you and me. He knows every one of us individually, and He cares about our lives. God loves us so much that after man rejected Him, He provided the means to get back to Him. He provided the means to have a wonderful relationship with Him. His love is available for all who would choose to receive it! *God does not want anyone to perish.*

Why do Christians want to share the Good News?

Christians want to share the Good News (the Gospel) because it is a commandment Jesus gave His disciples, and all Christians, just before He ascended back to Heaven. This is recorded in the book of

Matthew, chapter 28, verses 19 and 20. Jesus is speaking to His disciples:

> [18] And Jesus came and spoke to them, saying, "All authority has been given to Me in Heaven and on earth. [19] Go therefore and make disciples of all the nations, baptizing them in the name of the Father and of the Son and of the Holy Spirit, [20] teaching them to observe all things that I have commanded you; and lo, I am with you always, even to the end of the age." Amen.

You may be asking, "What is a disciple?" "What is baptizing?" and "What did Jesus' command mean?" Would you believe that even Christians ask some of these same questions? Before we get to those questions, Jesus is telling His disciples to make disciples, to baptize, and to teach them what Jesus has commanded (His teachings, His guidelines, His commandments). However, before anyone becomes a disciple, gets baptized, and even teaches others, they must first hear and understand the Good News and receive it. They must genuinely believe it. As we will discuss later, it is truly a matter of the heart.

In the Bible, in the book of Romans, chapter 10, verse 14, the question is asked: How can someone know Jesus if they have not heard of Him? The question continues by asking even deeper: How can they believe in Him if they have not heard of Him, and yet further, how can they hear of Him unless someone tells (preaches) about Him?

So, the first step in the process of becoming a Christian is hearing the Good News and believing it. From there, the question becomes, what kind of Christian will you be? This leads us to talk about being a disciple, baptism, and teaching.

It is said that a disciple of Jesus is a follower of Jesus. A follower of Jesus is an imitator of Jesus. Essentially, they practice a lifestyle that emulates the life of Jesus. Is that even possible in the world we live in today? Maybe. Does that mean that someone must be perfect? *No way.* Perfection is simply not possible on this side of Heaven.

Recall the Bible teaches that all people fall short of God's standard. They fall short of God's standard even while trying to live the most "Jesus-like," "Christ-like" lifestyle possible. This may sound hypocritical, but it is true. It is why you will sometimes hear Christians say that the church is full of hypocrites. It is true. The church is full of hypocrites. Outsiders of the church should understand that the church is nothing more than a hospital for Christians. The church is a hospital for sinners. It is where Christians go to learn, heal, and grow (get better).

Also, it is said that a disciple is a person who is perfecting their craft. In this case, the craft is learning and knowing more about Jesus, reaching new and deeper levels of faith, and living a lifestyle that pleases God by following His rules.

Baptism is an outward act of believing in Jesus and trusting Him for your salvation. We learn about baptism in the New Testament when a man named John the Baptist came on the scene. John the Baptist preceded Jesus' ministry and prepared the way for Jesus. Jesus sets the standard for baptism when John the Baptist baptizes Jesus.

The act of baptism emulates Jesus' death, burial, and resurrection. It is an important act of obedience to publicly express one's commitment to follow Jesus Christ. When a person is baptized and goes down under the water, the laying down and submersion process demonstrates death and burial. When a person is raised up out of the water, it demonstrates rising to a new life and being made into a new creation. A person can be baptized soon after they believe, or it can be a prolonged period before they are baptized. Some never get baptized. Most Christians agree that baptism is not a requirement to believe in Jesus and go to Heaven.

Once a person believes in Jesus and begins to learn more, they begin to participate in shaping their path in their Christian life. Everyone has different gifts and talents. This is true whether you are a Christian or not a Christian. However, Christians are constantly encouraged and reminded to follow Jesus' commandments, use their gifts, teach others, and to glorify Him.

Different Ways that Christians Share the Good News

John 3:16

One-way Christians share the Good News is simply by quoting one Bible verse, which is John, chapter 3, verse 16. This one Bible verse explains the Good News (the Gospel) about as concisely as possible. The passage is written again here:

> "FOR GOD SO LOVED THE WORLD THAT HE GAVE HIS ONLY BEGOTTEN SON, THAT WHOEVER BELIEVES IN HIM SHOULD NOT PERISH BUT HAVE EVERLASTING LIFE."

Telling the Bible Story

Another way Christians share the Good News (the Gospel) is by simply telling the Bible story. For those Christians who are gifted and motivated in evangelism, they learn to use this style depending upon how much time they have in talking with a non-believer. In other words, they can develop a short or longer version depending upon the amount of time. Here is an example of how this way of sharing the Good News may go.

> In the beginning, God created the Heavens and the earth. He created the Sun, Moon, Stars, and all the Universe. He created all the planets, including the Earth with the oceans, land, plants, animals, and all living things. He created man. The first man and woman were named Adam and Eve. They lived perfectly and in perfect harmony, with

God in the Garden of Eden. The world was perfect, and there was no sin.

God gave Adam and Eve dominion over all the earth and every living creature. They had everything they wanted and needed. However, God gave them one restriction. They could not eat from the tree of the knowledge of good and evil. This was a commandment.

Satan tempted Adam and Eve, and they disobeyed God. They ate the fruit from the tree of the knowledge of good and evil, and when they did, sin entered the world. Now, they knew the difference between good and evil. They became aware of their sin and knew that they had disobeyed God. Since sin had entered a perfect world, all of creation would now be subject to aging, decay, and death. Now, the perfect relationship that they had with God was broken.

How could the relationship between God and man be restored? Could man do something to get back to God or make things right with God? Only God could restore this kind of broken relationship.

So, God sent His Son, Jesus, into the world as a means for sinful man to be restored and reconciled to God. Jesus was born just like we are. He was not only fully God, but He was fully man. He lived a sinless life and obeyed all of God's laws.

God had to have payment for Adam and Eve's sin and all of mankind's sin. Jesus' death and resurrection on the cross was that payment. Jesus serves as our substitute. He died, was buried, and rose from the grave after three days. He is alive today and offers forgiveness of sin to anyone who believes in Him.

Bad News, Good News[6]

Another way Christians share the Good News (the Gospel) is through a style called *"Bad News, Good News."* Simply put, the bad news is that everyone is a sinner and cannot live up to God's standard. As a result, the consequences are death and eternal separation from God (in a place called Hell). The good news is that even though we are sinners, God loves us and sent Jesus to die for us. So, it is by God's Grace that we are saved through faith in Jesus. We are saved by God, not by anything we have done or can do. If we believe this, we will live forever and be with God forever (in a place called Heaven).

The Bible passages that tell us this are listed below. Passages are from the New King James Version (NKJV) translation.

- *Romans chapter 3, verse 23 says, "for all have sinned and fall short of the glory of God."*

- *Romans chapter 6, verse 23 says, "for the wages of sin is death."*

---

[6]R. Larry Moyer, *Evangelism, Sharing Christ in Contemporary Culture: Student Workbook, MIN507*, ed. Matt Smith (Winston-Salem, NC: Piedmont International University, 2014).

- *Romans chapter 5, verse 8 says, "But God demonstrates His own love toward us, in that while we were still sinners, Christ died for us."*

- *Ephesians chapter 2, verses 8 and 9 say, "For by grace you have been saved through faith, and that not of yourselves; it is a gift from God, not of works, lest anyone should boast."*

The Three Circles[7]

The 3 circles is a publication of the North American Mission Board (NAMB), which is part of the Southern Baptist Church (SBC). This is just one example of various organizations that write and publish ways to tell the Good News. Even individual Christians develop their own ways to convey the Good News message. Some use colorful bracelets and scarves where the colors direct the message. Regardless of what method or tool is used, the message is the same: Jesus is the way to forgiveness and eternal life.

The picture below shows 3 circles. The first circle is labeled as, "God's Design," the second circle is labeled as "Brokenness," and the third circle is labeled as "Gospel," which means the Good News.

---

[7] North American Mission Board, *The 3 Circles: Life Conversation Guide* (Alpharetta, GA: North American Mission Board, n.d.).

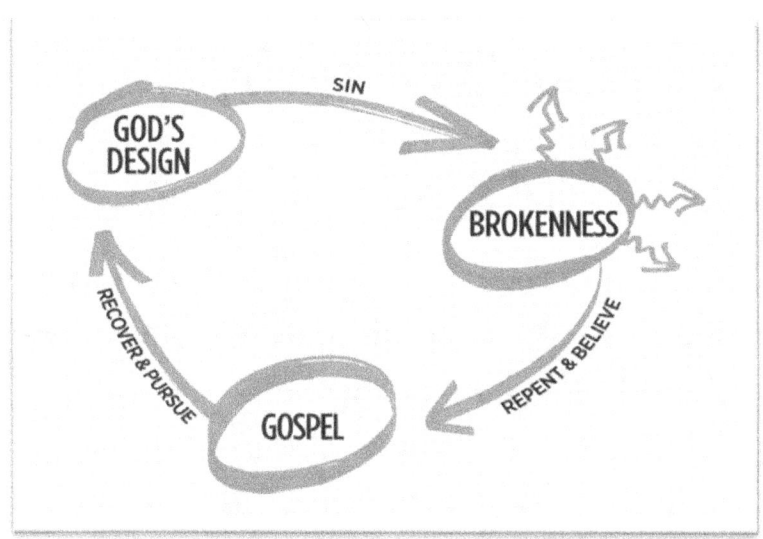

God's design was first, and it was perfect. Back in chapter 4, when God created the universe, the earth, and Adam and Eve, the Bible says that God concluded that it was good. There was no sin in the world, and God's relationship with Adam and Eve was perfect. However, the line with the arrow labeled "SIN" that is drawn across and points to the circle labeled Brokenness demonstrates that when sin entered the world, things became broken. The three squiggly lines represent various problems and issues we all have in our lives, ranging from personal relationships to health to downright sin in our lives.

But there is Good News. The line with the arrow labeled *"Repent and Believe"* that is drawn across and points to the circle labeled Gospel represents when a person realizes that they need Jesus. They realize that they are a sinner and cannot save themselves.

They hear the Good News that Jesus came to save them from their sins by dying in their place on a cross, being buried for three days, and rising on the third day. When a person believes the Gospel, their relationship with God is restored.

The line with the arrow labeled *"Recover and Pursue"* pointing back to God's Design is meant to depict that when a person receives Jesus and trusts in Him for their salvation, they are made right with God and can realize and pursue a more intimate relationship with God. They can truly know that even though they will one day come to the end of their life on earth, they will live with God and other believers in Heaven forever.

Sharing Their Own Story (Personal Testimony)

Christians share the Good News with non-believers by telling their own story. The pattern or structure that Christians use answers three basic questions:

- ✓ *What was my life like before I believed in Jesus?*
- ✓ *How did I come to believe in Jesus?*
- ✓ *What was/is my life like after I believed in Jesus?*

Christians will have their stories printed and use them to hand out (particularly as missionaries) when appropriate. Included with their own story are usually Bible passages that explain how someone becomes a Christian, how to connect with a local church, and individual contact information.

May I share my own personal story with you (my personal testimony)? I wanted to give you an example. Really, everything included in this book is to provide you with insight and basic information about Christianity, and even how Christians think. Even if you are not a Christian, you still have a story to tell. I want to encourage you to write your own story down on paper. Rather than the questions about Jesus above, what if the three questions you used went something like this?

✓ *What was my life like when I was a younger person?*

✓ *What has happened in my life that really changed me/changed my direction?*

✓ *How is life now for me, and what do I want my future to look like?*

Here is My Personal Story/Testimony

Hello, my name is Stephen Jumper, and I am from North Carolina. I am so excited to be with you to share my story, but even more filled with joy to tell you about the most important thing, the most important person in my life, Jesus Christ.

I was fortunate as a child that my parents took me to church, gave me a Bible, and taught me that if I believe

Jesus Christ died and rose from the dead to save me from my sins, I will live with HIM in Heaven forever.

In 2002, my first wife told me she wanted a divorce. With a family and 2 daughters, I was devastated. It was the worst time in my life. It would be only by the Grace of God that I would make it through. I totally surrendered my life to Christ again. And God began to rebuild my life.

I studied the Bible more than ever and began ministering to those who had experienced divorce. Also, I began traveling to Russia and Southeast Asia on some incredible mission trips where I witnessed to and saw thousands of people hearing about Jesus for the first time and accepting HIM as Lord and Savior. Through my trips and Bible study, I was led back to school for a Master of Ministry in 2016.

Also, God reconciled my personal life in an unbelievable way. In 2014, I married my wife Charlotte, who has 2 grown daughters and 4 grandchildren, along with several other family members who live locally. Suddenly, I was surrounded by family and the love of 2 beautiful granddaughters and 2 awesome grandsons.

When I think of how God restored me both spiritually and personally, I cannot help but think about how God restored Job in the Old Testament. Also, my wife and I have dedicated ourselves to loving the LORD and using HIS Word, the Bible, to guide our lives. We have written Ecclesiastes 4:12 in our hearts and use it as our marriage verse: *"Though one may be overpowered by another, two can withstand him. And a threefold cord is not quickly broken."*

That third strand is JESUS CHRIST—Let me tell you about HIM!!

Chapter 7

Don't Cut the Grass on Sunday!

I have lived most of my life in the South. Originally, my family roots are in South Carolina, where I had grandparents who were members of the Lutheran Church, and the other grandparents were members of the Southern Baptist Church (SBC – the Southern Baptist Church).

While we discuss different church denominations in the next chapter, let's talk further about the contrast between the Lutheran and SBC. To put it simply, the Lutheran Church was based on the Catholic Church, while the SBC was more biblically based, following the literal teachings of the Bible.

While my parents raised me in the Lutheran church, I was fortunate as a child to attend my grandparents' SBC when we visited in the summer times in the 1970s. This gave me exposure to the contrasting style of the two church services, but more impactful was what I learned from my grandparents, who attended there.

Back then, the SBC was still practicing a style of worship and preaching commonly known as "fire and brimstone." The basic message of the "fire and brimstone" style of church was that if you don't turn from your sins, you are "bound straight to the gates of Hell." These are harsh words for a Christian, much less someone who is a non-believer. If you are not from the South and unfamiliar with how it was in the "Bible Belt" in the mid-1900s, this style of preaching was prominent in the SBC. The Bible Belt was considered the most southern states in the South and Southeast, which were usually composed of mostly Southern Baptist Churches. As time has evolved and the culture in America has shifted, the SBC has moved away from this style of worship in general. There are still some smaller churches that worship this way, though.

I recall one summer Sunday night attending a worship service. The preacher was fired up. I do not know what the sermon was about, but all I can remember is that when people were leaving the church, there was a lot of commotion, and there were many who were crying and emotional. The most important thing for me was that I could definitely tell the difference between the two church denominations.

My SBC grandparents had read their Bible, and they knew what the Bible said. When we visited, they would teach it to me and my sister. All kinds of ideas and topics would come up through the years. In addition, we were able to observe their habits and lifestyle.

For example, we quickly learned what they believed about going to church on Sunday because of how they dealt with what the Bible teaches about the Sabbath, God's Day of rest. As the week was winding down towards Friday and Saturday, things seemed to focus on doing everything to get ready for Sunday.

On Saturday, my grandmother would do most of her cooking for Sunday. She still cooked maybe one dish on Sunday, but it was a simple one. The rest of the food could just be heated up. My grandmother would do all her shopping and laundry on Saturday. My grandfather would check on his cattle and make sure the farm was dealt with, so that he did not have to go out and work on Sunday. If there was any work around the house that needed to be done, it either got done during the week or on Saturday. It seemed that as Sunday drew closer, the focus was on getting the chores done, so you could go to church on Sunday and rest.

If you are not from the South, I will have to tell you that this is considered a "southern" philosophy. You could say it was just how life was in the South. More than philosophically, it was biblical for those who honestly believed and wanted to follow what the Bible says.

So, here is the back story for the title of this book. When I got old enough to start helping my grandfather tend to his cows and help out around their farm with various chores, he would slowly give me more responsibility. He had a riding lawnmower that he used to cut their almost 2-acre front and back yard. What teenager does not want to learn how to drive the lawnmower (at that age, I was calling it a full-fledged tractor), and ride around the yard for the day? I loved it! I felt so grown up and appreciated how my grandfather trusted me to take care of that chore. Besides teaching all about how the lawnmower worked and entrusting me with even more chores as I got older, he added one important lesson about all the work that needed to be done around the house. Because the week, and particularly Saturday, involved getting all your work done before Sunday came, my grandfather always said, "Don't Cut the Grass on Sunday."

He would talk about this one chore, and it stood out as an outward sign to be respectful of God's Day of rest on Sunday. He would talk about the neighbors and what they would think if they saw him cutting the grass on Sunday. Obviously, it really stuck with me, and for my entire life, I have always thought it would make a great title for a book.

But what would the book be about? What would the topic be? The question was always about choosing the subject matter. Would it be about Sunday and everything the Bible says about the Sabbath day? Since the Sabbath commandment is one of the Ten Commandments, would it be about the entire Ten Commandments? I thought a book like that might not be appealing, and difficult to both write and read. Write about just one of the Ten Commandments, "Remember the Sabbath day by keeping it Holy." How much could I write about the Sabbath, about Sunday? A book on the Ten Commandments could be stiff and boring.

While I considered authoring a book with this title most of my life, it was not until I started to grow in my own personal beliefs about God over the past twenty years. It was the life events in my own life that have influenced me to consider several different topics. The events that have influenced me most were my divorce in 2003, my first mission/business trip to Russia in 2011, and the overseas mission trips to Southeast Asia in 2013, which included the Philippines, Thailand, Malaysia, and Cambodia. Other influences in my life were reading the Bible in its entirety several times, going back to school and getting a master's degree in ministry, and working in various ministry organizations.

In 2016, as I was finishing my ministry degree, I began to conceptualize and outline a draft of *"Don't Cut the Grass on Sunday."* However, focusing on the Sabbath, the Ten Commandments, and more serious theological approaches, it became extremely academic and more like a book on Apologetics. Apologetics means "defending the Christian faith." Over the course of 2016 and 2017, I could see that this was not where *"Don't Cut the Grass on Sunday"* should focus. I would say I piddled around with this and other ideas for a couple of years and even put the idea aside until 2025.

In recent years, most of the mission trips I have taken have been in the United States. Because of these trips across America, I started to notice how "church people" talked to "non-church" people. I noticed how Christians were quick to throw down their viewpoints to non-Christians. They would assume that non-Christians knew the "lingo" and would move too quickly with their approach. I noticed how Christians were "preachy" and would/could become argumentative very quickly.

As I gained experience sharing the Good News (the Gospel) with non-believers, I recognized that each person was unique. I could see that each had a different story to tell. Some knew little or nothing about God and the Bible, while others had some knowledge and experience; still, others had the WRONG knowledge and experience. Please do not misunderstand. What I mean by having the WRONG knowledge is simply being misinformed or not knowing what the Bible honestly says, or what the Christian faith is truly about. What I mean by having the WRONG experience is simply having an UNPLEASANT experience. This would happen by having a negative exposure to church lifestyle or encountering a Christian that was not a genuinely nice Christian, and simply not a nice person.

I was able to take some time off in the first few months of 2025 and revisit my thoughts about *"Don't Cut the Grass on Sunday."* Going back to my consideration that the Sabbath was one of the Ten Commandments, I thought about how non-Christians must view Christianity as rigid and full of nothing but rules, like not doing any work on Sunday. Did they know that Jesus actually healed people on the Sabbath and was accused of breaking the Sabbath Law because they considered healing to be work? I considered that some non-Christians thought these types of commandments were restrictive and limiting to one's lifestyle. I have even been exposed to non-believers, thinking that Christianity does not look like it would be much fun.

Also, I considered how sharing the Good News (the Gospel) in America was so difficult. How could such a book title tie into Jesus' story and plan of salvation? I considered even how the title would tie into and include many Bible basics. Given that most non-Christians would likely look at a book title like *"Don't Cut the Grass on Sunday"* and think, "Oh great, another Christian book about following rules."

Thinking through all this led me back to the Good News and that maybe a more straightforward approach was needed about not only sharing the Good News but about Bible basics that were explained with a layman's style instead of some "churchy," particularly "preachy" way. As I researched and looked for books written like this, I found very few, or possibly not even one.

So, let's discuss the Bible principle behind *"Don't Cut the Grass on Sunday."* Remember, *there is a Commandment here,* and I do want to touch on it briefly. In the book of Exodus (the second book in the Bible, Old Testament), God gives Moses the Ten Commandments. Included in the Ten Commandments is the fourth commandment concerning the Sabbath day. In Exodus chapter 20, verses 8-11, God says:

> [8] "Remember the Sabbath day, to keep it holy. [9] Six days you shall labor, and do all your work, [10] but the seventh day is the Sabbath of the LORD your God. In it, you shall not do any work, you, nor your son, nor your daughter, nor your male servant, or your female servant, nor your cattle, nor your stranger who is within your gates. [11] For in six days the LORD made the heavens and the earth, the sea, and all that is in them, and rested the seventh day. Therefore, the LORD blessed the Sabbath day and hallowed it."

If we consider the creation account back in Genesis (the first book of the Bible—Old Testament), it says that God made the Earth and all creation in six days and on the seventh day He rested. Now, if God is truly an all-powerful, all-knowing, omnipotent being, does He really need to rest? Did He rest? Whether He rested or not, He did not need it, but He was setting an example. He provided order for man in this new creation and cared for man by providing a day that man needed, not God. If you have ever worked too much and not taken a day off, you know what I mean. Having a day off to get re-energized for another week is something we all could agree that we need.

So, in the Jewish custom, Sunday was the first day of the week (a working day), and Saturday was the seventh day of the week, which is why the Jewish nation celebrated their Sabbath from sundown on Friday until sundown on Saturday. In the next chapter, we will touch upon how this custom was changed when the Roman Catholic Church was established in the early sixth century.

The Jewish leadership had taken this Sabbath commandment to the extreme and turned it into something that was a burden, rather than the blessing it was intended to be. This became extremely evident during Jesus' time and ministry. The Jewish leaders would accuse its people of working on the Sabbath when they were going about their most basic tasks. Some of the things the Jewish people did on the Sabbath as a means of essential daily living could be considered a form of work by the Jewish leaders.

The Jewish leadership accused Jesus of breaking the law when He healed people on the Sabbath. One of the reasons why they accused Jesus of this was that they were looking to have Him arrested and ultimately put to death. The Bible provides several accounts of this.

Jesus' response was extremely spiritual but practical. He questioned the Jewish leadership and asked them if it was unlawful to do good on the Sabbath. Also, He brought their position into question when He asked about what they would do if their ox had fallen into a ditch on the Sabbath day. From the book of Luke, chapter 14, verse 5:

5 Then He answered them, saying, *"Which of you, having a donkey or an ox that has fallen into a pit, will not immediately pull him out on the Sabbath day?"*

Essentially, Jesus was asking them if they would pull their livestock out or let it die just because it was the Sabbath day.

Many non-Christians think that Christianity is about a bunch of rules that must be followed, and it restricts people from doing the necessary things in their day-to-day lives. The fourth commandment concerning the Sabbath and Jesus' examples of doing good demonstrate that it's not as straightforward as you think. For most things like this one, it is a matter of the HEART. The Bible tells us that God knows our hearts. He wants us to trust Him, be honest with Him, and have an open, sincere relationship with Him.

Have I ever cut the grass on Sunday? You betcha! Now, do I try to take my grandfather's advice and not cut the grass on Sunday? You betcha! When you think about several vital services that are essential, like doctors, nurses, fire, and police officers, does everyone have to take their Sabbath on Sunday? Can a person's Sabbath day be on another day of the week besides Sunday?

The times I remember when I felt like I had to cut the grass on Sunday were usually weather-related, or I was going out of town for an extended period. At times, it would rain for several days in a row, and the grass would grow high. Sunday would be a beautiful day, but I was leaving town early on Monday morning to travel. If I needed the yard to look good for out-of-town guests, maybe I would cut the grass on Sunday. In any case, for most of my life, I have worked hard to follow my grandfather's direction, "**Don't Cut the Grass on Sunday.**"

Chapter 8

What's Up with the Church?

I'm going to assume that, as a non-Christian or Christian skeptic, you understand that Christians meet in what is known as the church. However, the church is more than a building or a place to worship and learn about God. The church is a group of people who are believers in Jesus Christ and are considered "a body" of people or "a body" of believers.

In this chapter, when I speak about the church, please understand that it is the group of people or Christian community that I am referring to, and not simply a building. The concept of "the church" in this context is important to understand because it helps us learn more about God and what His intentions are for His followers and believers as part of "the church body."

The Early Church

During Jesus' ministry, He was having a conversation with His disciples. His question to them was, "Who do people say that I am?" In other words, He was asking His disciples what people thought about Him and who He was. Jesus heard several answers from His disciples, but the one that stood out was Peter's response. It is recorded in the book of Matthew, chapter 16, verses 16–18.

> [16] Simon Peter answered and said, "You are the Christ, the Son of the living God." [17] Jesus answered and said to him, "Blessed are you, Simon Bar-Jonah, for flesh and blood has not revealed *this* to you, but My Father who is in Heaven. [18] And I also say to you that you are Peter, and on this rock, I will build My church, and the gates of Hades shall not prevail against it."

As a result of this conversation, Jesus' disciple Peter is often referred to as "The Rock." However, when Jesus explains that He will build His church "on this rock," He means that He will build His church on the proclamation that Peter made, not on Peter himself. The proclamation that Jesus is the Christ, or Messiah, and the Son of the living God is the foundation of the church today.

Jesus is considered and proclaimed to be the "Head of the Church." Peter is credited with being the leader of the church movement. In addition, this is evidenced by the sermon that Peter preaches after Jesus returns to Heaven.

Jesus spent forty days on earth after His resurrection. After these forty days, the Bible teaches that He "ascended" into Heaven and sat down at the right hand of God the Father. Before He ascended, though, He gave the disciples an important commandment. He told them to go tell others about Him. He told them to go spread "the Word." He told them to go and share the

"Good News." Again, this passage is recorded in the book of Matthew, chapter 28, verses 19–20. Additionally, it is included later in the book in the chapter entitled *"Going Deeper: Essential Spiritual Beliefs,"* because Christians call this The Great Commission.

> [19] Go therefore and make disciples of all the nations, baptizing them in the name of the Father and of the Son and of the Holy Spirit, [20] teaching them to observe all things that I have commanded you; and lo, I am with you always, *even* to the end of the age." Amen.

So, after Jesus ascended back to Heaven, it was time for His disciples to follow through on Jesus' command. They needed to get organized and begin this ministry of telling others about Jesus. The plan for them was to follow Jesus' instruction of starting the church.

Jesus' instruction to the disciples after His ascension back to Heaven was to go to Jerusalem and wait ten days for the "Helper," the Holy Spirit. This is an incredibly important event in the history of the church. The church refers to this event as Pentecost.

If we take a step back and look at God's overall plan, as documented in the Bible, we can see that in the Old Testament, it was primarily God the Father who dealt directly with His people. The Bible describes that, just at the right time in history, Jesus came. It says that Jesus came "in the fullness of time," and lived here on earth as fully God and fully man for approximately thirty-three years. When Jesus ascended back into Heaven, He told His disciples that it was to their advantage that He go away. God the Father would send the "Helper," the Holy Spirit, to live in them and provide insight and power to spread the Good News of Jesus' forgiveness on the cross and the promise of eternal salvation.

After the disciples had received the Holy Spirit, Peter then preached to a large crowd of thousands of people publicly in Jerusalem. While the sermon is quite long and recounts the life and authority of Jesus, its message is simply the Good News which we have talked about before: "repent, believe, and be saved."

As a result of Peter's sermon, more than five thousand came to believe in Jesus. If it was five thousand men that came to believe in Jesus because of Peter's preaching, it means that the total number of new believers could have been much higher, since it did not account for women and youth. This is considered to be the beginning of the Church Age.

Also, because of this sermon, and with more public preaching by all the disciples, the church in Jerusalem was persecuted by the Jewish leaders. As a result of this persecution, the church grew and spread out to other parts of Israel.

The disciples began to travel outside of Jerusalem to tell others about Jesus' resurrection and His gift of salvation if they believed.

As the church was being persecuted and spread across the region, another important figure emerged. His name was Saul. Saul had been one of those Jewish leaders who persecuted the church. He approved of and witnessed the martyrdom of the first Christian named Stephen, who was stoned to death. Saul was a devout Jew who was well educated in Jewish beliefs and customs. He fought to maintain those Jewish traditions and to eradicate the movement of the Christian faith (the Jesus movement, also known as "The Way," at the time). Personally, Saul killed many Christians.

As he was traveling to Damascus in the northern region of Israel to kill more Christians, Jesus appeared and confronted Saul. Today, Christians refer to this encounter as the "Road to Damascus" experience. In this encounter, Saul was knocked off his horse and blinded. Jesus appeared to him in a great light and asked Saul why he was persecuting Him. Jesus told Saul that He was Jesus. Jesus told Saul to go into the city of Damascus and wait. So, his traveling companions took him into the city, where he remained blind and did not eat or drink for three days.

God spoke to and sent a man named Ananias to Saul to restore his eyesight and so that he might receive the Holy Spirit. The Bible tells us that as Ananias laid hands on Saul, something like scales fell from his eyes. His sight was restored, and Saul received the Holy Spirit.

Saul was a changed man. He went from being a non-believer in Jesus and a persecutor of Christians to being one of the greatest evangelists of all time. He spent time with local disciples of Jesus in Damascus and began to preach the Good News of Jesus' resurrection and His plan of salvation for the world. He spent several years studying with disciples and others who had been close to Jesus when He was alive. As a reflection of this incredible transformation, Saul's name was changed to Paul.

Part of Jesus' instruction to the disciples was to first take the message of the Good News to the Jewish nation, and then secondly, to nations that were non-Jewish, like Greeks and Romans. The Bible refers to all non-Jewish people, including Greeks, Romans, and the rest of the world, and calls them Gentiles.

As Jesus' disciples and Paul entered a town to preach, they would first stop at the Jewish temple or synagogue while the Jews were having their daily worship services and teachings. Afterwards, they would encounter the rest of the people in the local community and share the Good News.

While Christianity was spreading and more believers were coming to know who Jesus was, there remained tremendous resistance among the Jewish people to preserve their long-established beliefs and traditions. One of the most critical turns in church history occurred in a town called Antioch (today just north of the Syrian border in modern-day Türkiye). The Jews rejected Paul's message in the synagogue in Antioch. As a result, Paul proclaimed that he would now take the message of the Good News to the Gentiles. The Bible recounts that Jesus had established this when He encountered Paul on the road to Damascus, and now, at this turning point in church history, Paul was proclaiming it.

As a result of the Jews rejecting Jesus and Paul taking the Good News (the Gospel) to the Gentiles, the established church in Antioch was where followers of Jesus were first called Christians. As previously mentioned, the Jesus movement had been referred to as "The Way."

Paul became one of the most, if not the most, impactful disciples of Jesus. The Bible tells us about Paul's four important missionary journeys across the region. On these journeys, Paul encountered incredible levels of obstacles and suffering. Paul was beaten, shipwrecked, and imprisoned many times for his efforts to share Jesus and the Good News. Eventually, Paul ended up in Rome, Italy, and along with Peter, helped establish the church there.

Paul is credited with writing most of the New Testament and establishing churches all over the Middle East and Mediterranean regions. He is considered the most influential and prominent figure in establishing the church and the growth of Christianity around the world. His life would end when he was martyred in Rome.

All the disciples traveled across the Middle East and Mediterranean regions, preaching and establishing local churches. All of them, except John, were martyred for their preaching and faith in Jesus. John died a natural death in isolation on the island of Patmos in the Mediterranean Sea. Following is a list of the disciples,[8] where they traveled, and how they died. One of the defenses of the Christian faith begs the question, why would men die for something that they didn't see happen or something that was made up? This is a question beyond the scope of this book, but I consider it important to mention.

- **James (Jesus' half-brother)** was the first disciple to die. He died by the sword under King Herod in Jerusalem.

- **Peter** was crucified upside down in Rome around 66 AD under Emperor Nero.

- **John** ministered around Ephesus. He died a natural death on the island of Patmos.

- **Andrew** traveled to modern-day Russia, Türkiye, and Greece. He was martyred there.

---

[8] Faith on Hill Church, "What Happened to the 12 Disciples?" Faith on Hill Church (blog), February 11, 2020, https://www.faithonhill.com/blog/what-happened-to-the-12-disciples.

- **Philip** ministered in North Africa and Asia Minor. He was martyred.

- **Bartholomew** traveled to Ethiopia, Armenia, and the Arabian regions. He was martyred.

- **Matthew** traveled to Iran and Ethiopia. He was stabbed to death in Africa.

- **Thomas** traveled to India. He died by stabbing at the hands of four soldiers.

- **James (John's brother)** traveled to the regions north of Israel. He was stoned and clubbed to death.

- **Simon the Zealot** was sawed in half in Persia.

- **Thaddeus** traveled to northern Iraq and Türkiye. He was martyred.

- **Matthias** traveled to the Caspian Sea. He was martyred.

Because of the spread of the Good News, Italy would become a Christian nation. This was another critical point in church history. The beginnings of the Roman Catholic Church started in A.D. 590, under Gregory I, and a consolidation of church and political power was established. Under Catholic rule, various beliefs were established about the role of the Church. The Church, under

Catholic doctrine, took on a more heightened, powerful, and political role.[9]

One of the beliefs of the Catholic Church was the role of the priest when it came to a person's relationship with God and their forgiveness of sins. The Catholic Church established that the priest served as an intermediary between God and the sinner. It was necessary that the sinner meet with the priest, confess their sins to him, and that the priest had the power to forgive the person's sins. Part of this belief comes from the Old Testament in the Bible, where the priests in Israel interceded for the Jewish nation to ask God for forgiveness through various sacrifices.

The Bible teaches that there is only one High Priest, and His name is Jesus. Because of Jesus' death, burial, and resurrection for the remission of sins, a person has direct access to God. While the Bible documents and provides for various roles in the church, because of Jesus' atoning sacrifice, we can have a direct relationship with God. Prayer, Bible study, and fellowship with other believers, by the work of the Holy Spirit, are how a person strengthens their relationship with God.

The doctrines and beliefs of the Roman Catholic Church are wide-ranging, and controversy exists today in many of these areas.

---

[9] Paul Enns, *The Moody Handbook of Theology* (Chicago: Moody Publishers, 2008), 567.

The Church defines the role of the Papacy (the Pope), Mary (the mother of Jesus), Purgatory (a holding place when one dies), the Sacraments (Ceremonies), Marriage, and Baptism (Catholics baptize infants by sprinkling), just to name a few. While Emperor Constantine first moved the Sabbath from Saturday to Sunday early on, when Rome became a Christian nation, the Roman Catholic Church sanctioned it as well. Contemporary practices of the modern-day church consider that Jesus rose on the first day of the week; hence, today's tradition of Sunday being the Sabbath day.[10]

Through the early centuries, the Roman Catholic Church had established its authority and, even more so, control over the people. A man named Martin Luther was born in 1483. As a student, he studied the Bible and intended to become a Catholic monk. However, he became disillusioned with the corruption he saw in the Catholic Church and, through divine revelation, came to the knowledge of justification by faith alone,[11] as seen in the book of Romans, chapter 1, verses 16–17. The Apostle Paul writes:

> [16] For I am not ashamed of the gospel of Christ, for it is the power of God to salvation for everyone who believes, for the Jew first and also for the Greek. [17] For in it the righteousness of God is revealed from faith to faith; as it is written, "The just shall live by faith."

---

[10] "How The Sabbath Was Changed," *Sabbath Truth*, Amazing Facts International Media Ministry, accessed September 25, 2025, https://www.sabbathtruth.com/sabbath-history/how-the-sabbath-was-changed.

[11] Paul Enns, *The Moody Handbook of Theology* (Chicago: Moody Publishers, 2008), 472.

It was Martin Luther's belief that the Roman Catholic Church had distorted the view of salvation as a free gift from God for those who would believe and have faith in Jesus. Rather than a works-based religion, Martin Luther believed that Christians are justified by their faith in Jesus Christ alone. On October 31, 1517, Martin Luther nailed the Ninety-five Theses to the door of the Catholic Church at Wittenberg, Germany.[12] This is known as the beginning of the Protestant Reformation.

While Martin Luther intended to reform the Catholic Church, his action in 1517 produced a movement called Lutheranism and established the Lutheran Church. The Lutheran Church is considered the first Protestant Church, and it produced additional movements led by various men. John Calvin and John Knox are credited with starting the Presbyterian Church. John Wesley, along with his brother Charles Wesley, is credited with establishing the Methodist Church. John Smyth and John Helwys are credited with starting the Baptist Church. Many other church denominations exist today, including the Episcopal Church and the Moravian Church. These different churches are referred to as denominations.

As these church denominations grew initially in Europe, they were eventually brought to North America. The Roman Catholic

---

[12] Paul Enns, *The Moody Handbook of Theology* (Chicago: Moody Publishers, 2008), 472.

Church was one of the earliest denominations. Other denominations that followed were the Lutherans, Quakers, Moravians, Methodists, and Baptists, not necessarily in that order. As the United States of America was emerging, the church saw its role as a vital part of shaping the belief and cultural foundation of a new and developing country. As you probably know and have heard Christians say today, they believe that America was founded on Judeo-Christian principles.

Because of the Judeo-Christian influence, Christianity grew in America, and up until just recently, America was considered a Christian nation. For a period, it could be said that most of America was Christian and had a common value system based on biblical principles.

Today, it is fair to say that Christianity has lost ground in America. As seen recently, church attendance is on the decline, and while many different viewpoints are making headway, it could be said that it's actually the church in America itself that is to blame. As other religions, like Islam, and various social viewpoints have challenged Christianity, it could be considered a fact that the church itself has been in retreat. While the Bible would say that marriage and sexuality are Christian issues, politics and social viewpoints have grabbed those issues and used them to advance other cultural aspects of life in America. While the culture has wanted to address these biblical concepts, the church in America has failed to stand up and defend what it believes and what the Bible says. Misinformation has permeated our culture and distorted what the Bible says about these topics. The church should reestablish its role in society and be motivated more than ever to fight to take back its cultural ground, working with people of all beliefs in a more straightforward, plain-spoken way.

Chapter 9

Going Deeper: Basic & Essential Christian Beliefs

This chapter will list, break down, and summarize the core beliefs of Christianity. These beliefs produce a lifestyle considered to make a person a Christian. However, according to the Bible, there is only one belief that determines whether you will spend eternity in Heaven or Hell. Do you believe that you are a sinner, cannot save yourself, and are sorry for your sins? Will you ask for forgiveness and believe that Jesus died and rose from the dead as your Savior? While this one thing is the most important, there are other essential spiritual beliefs.

Christians who have been believers most of their lives seem to complicate the Christian faith unnecessarily, particularly when it comes to each denomination of the church, as we have discussed previously. Even so, Christians are not good at breaking down their faith and, moreover, not really that good at explaining it to someone else.

The following Christian beliefs are based on what the Bible says. Most of them are listed on a Christian organization's website. Most churches will list them and call them Doctrinal Statements. It is important for Christians and non-Christians alike to know what these are if they are involved in a church or other organization. It can even be confusing within the scope of so many different church denominations. Some churches will list them, and other churches will only list a select few. Essentially, they are considered Christian churches, but do not adhere to the same core Christian beliefs.

You may ask, how can each church "pick and choose"? To which I would say, that is a particularly good question, and one that is continually debated within the Christian community. *However, if a church considers itself Christian, it is irrefutable that they believe in the life, death, and resurrection of Jesus Christ for the remission of their sins and eternal salvation.* If they do not believe this, then they are not Christian, and all their other belief statements come into question.

The following is a list of core beliefs in the Bible. They are not necessarily presented in the Bible in the order in which I am listing them. I will talk about each and attempt to provide an explanation of where they fall in relation to their importance and essentiality. Some build upon one another, while others stand independently. I will attempt to explain that as I talk about them.

Believe in Jesus: A Matter of the Heart

Now, before you start "punching" your first-class ticket to Heaven just by believing that Jesus existed, let's talk about something called "a matter of the heart." The "matter of the heart" speaks about what a person genuinely believes inside themselves. The heart is defined as the seat of our emotions and the essence of who we are. It is commonly referred to as "the soul." People can talk all day about what they believe, but do they sincerely, genuinely believe it? Do their beliefs find their way deep within themselves, reaching heart and soul?

Is there someone who really knows what you believe in your heart? Do you know what you believe in your own heart, actually?

The authors of most books in the New Testament document that believing in Jesus will result in eternal life in Heaven. To provide you with the most essential understanding and example, let me point you to the book of John, one of the four books called the Gospels. In the book of John, Jesus is consoling His friend Martha because her brother Lazarus has just died. He tells Martha that He (Jesus) is "the resurrection and the life." He continues to tell her that anyone who believes in Him (Jesus) will not die, but that they will live forever.

So, we must ask the question, "What does it mean to believe in Jesus?" I realize that there are other questions that, as a non-believer, you may ask. Do I believe that Jesus even actually existed and was a real person? Is the Bible a historical book that documents actual events? Is there more historical evidence that Jesus actually walked on the earth?

For now, let me ask you to set aside these additional questions and consider what it means to simply "believe in Jesus." This is an important question not only for non-Christians but also one that is extremely important in the Christian community. I can tell you that there are many people in and out of the church today who say they believe in Jesus but are not Christians. While yes, the Bible teaches that to believe is to be saved, there is much more explanation needed.

The best way to explain this is to share the account of Jesus' crucifixion on the cross. As mentioned in an earlier chapter, when Jesus was crucified, He was crucified between two other men. These men were criminals who had committed heinous crimes. These men are called "the thieves on the cross" in the Bible.

When a person is crucified, their body is stretched out, and their hands and feet are nailed to the cross. When the cross is raised vertically, pressure is exerted on the lungs from the person's own weight, and their breathing is restricted, requiring them to push up with their feet and legs to inhale and exhale. It is a slow, gruesome, painful death, resulting in the person ultimately suffocating because they become too weak to push themselves up to breathe.

Given the fact that Jesus hung on the cross for three hours and went through this process, all three men were able to speak to one another. One of the thieves mocked Jesus and said that if He was really the King of the Jews, He should save Himself and both of them. The other thief defended Jesus and said that Jesus had done nothing wrong. He said that they (the two thieves) both deserved to die, but that Jesus had done nothing wrong and was innocent. In the book of Luke, chapter 23, verse 42, finally, this thief addressed Jesus and said, "Lord, remember me when you come into your Kingdom."

Wow, simple words, right? What did that mean? What was the thief asking, and certainly, what did he mean by the word "remember"?

What occurred next is perhaps even more remarkable. In the very next passage of Luke, chapter 23, verse 43, Jesus answered this thief directly and said, "*Assuredly, I say to you, today you will be with Me in Paradise.*"

Jesus knew this thief's heart. The Bible doesn't tell us, but we have to assume that Jesus knew much more than we do from reading this account. The thief was a thief. I am guessing he did not spend his life doing mostly "good things" and likely spent his life doing unbelievably dreadful things. So how could he, just by asking Jesus to "remember him," go to Heaven? This is a question that many articles and commentaries have explored. I do believe that Jesus knew this thief's heart and that the man had surrendered it all to Jesus' authority and lordship, crying out to Jesus to save him.

Here's how the actual Bible puts it in the book of Luke, chapter 23, verses 39–43, from the Easy English translation:

> [39] One of the bad men on a cross at the side of Jesus started to insult him. He shouted, "You say that you are the Messiah, don't you? Then save your own life and save our lives too!"
> [40] But the bad man on the other cross told him that he should be quiet. He said, "You should be more afraid of God. We will die here, as well as him. [41] We two men have done very bad things. So, it is right that we should die. But this man has not done anything wrong." [42] Then the man said to Jesus, "Remember me, Jesus, when you start to rule in your kingdom." [43] Jesus replied, "I promise you, today you will be with me in paradise."

Believe in Jesus: A Matter of Eternal Life

The Bible clearly tells us that if a person believes that they are a sinner and that Jesus died and rose from the dead to pay the price for their sin, they will be saved and have eternal life in Heaven. The Bible teaches that because you believe this one thing, you will go to Heaven and live with God forever. This is believing in Jesus Christ, and it is called the Gospel and the Good News. Remember, the word "Gospel" is a Greek word that means "Good News." Here are a few passages from the Bible that many Christians refer to when they want to tell someone what this belief is based on.

In the book of John, chapter 14, verse 6:

[6] Jesus said to him, *"I am the way, the truth, and the life.* No one comes to the Father except through Me."

In the book of Ephesians, chapter 2, verses 8–9:

[8] *For by grace you have been saved through faith,* and that not of yourselves; it is the gift of God; [9] not of works, lest anyone should boast.

In the book of John, chapter 3, verses 16–18:

[16] For God so loved the world that He gave His only begotten Son, that whoever believes in Him should not perish but have everlasting life. [17] For God did not send His Son into the world to condemn the world, but that the world through Him might be saved. [18] "He who believes in Him is not condemned, but he who does not believe is condemned already, because he has not believed in the name of the only begotten Son of God."

In the book of Acts, chapter 4, verses 11–12:

[11] "This is the 'stone which was rejected by you builders, which has become the chief cornerstone.' [12] Nor is there salvation in any other, for there is no other name under Heaven given among men by which we must be saved."

The Unpardonable Sin

The Bible tells us that there is one sin that is unpardonable. *How can a God who is supposed to be a God of love and forgiveness define a sin that He cannot forgive? How is that possible?* On the surface, it sounds contradictory.

This is a good example of many things that people hear about Christianity and jump to quick conclusions without much research or study. Even for me in my younger years, I would hear things in church or through other Christians that were confusing and did not make sense. When anyone first reads the Bible, it can sound complicated. It is not until someone really reads it thoroughly, compares various scriptures, and frankly works with a knowledgeable and experienced person to fully understand some biblical concepts.

Simply put, the unpardonable sin is blasphemy against the Holy Spirit.

What is blasphemy? From the website "dictionary.com," blasphemy is defined as "an impious utterance or action concerning God or sacred things; an act of cursing or reviling God; the crime of assuming oneself the right or qualities of God; and irreverent behavior toward anything held sacred."[13]

Recall back in the chapter entitled "Basics Before the Basics," I discussed how both the Bible and the Holy Spirit work together to help a person come to faith in Jesus Christ. When the Holy Spirit is working with a person, the Holy Spirit is actually offering that

---

[13] "Blasphemy," Dictionary.com,
<<Link:https://www.dictionary.com/browse/blasphemy
https://www.dictionary.com/browse/blasphemy>>, (accessed August 1, 2025).

person the opportunity to come to faith in Jesus. You could say that the Holy Spirit is inviting them. *When the Holy Spirit invites someone to have a relationship with Jesus, He is inviting that person to believe in God.*

When the person misses the opportunity through apathy or rejects the Holy Spirit's invitation, that is considered blasphemy against the Holy Spirit. In other words, when a person chooses not to accept Jesus and not to believe in God, it is considered "unbelief." This "unbelief" is considered blasphemy against the Holy Spirit. Here are two Bible verses that define the unpardonable sin.

Matthew, chapter 12, verses 31–32:

[31] "Therefore, I say to you, every sin and blasphemy will be forgiven men, but the blasphemy *against* the Spirit will not be forgiven men. [32] Anyone who speaks a word against the Son of Man, it will be forgiven him; but whoever speaks against the Holy Spirit, it will not be forgiven him, either in this age or in the age to come."

Mark, chapter 3, verses 28–29:

[28] "Assuredly, I say to you, all sins will be forgiven the sons of men, and whatever blasphemies they may utter; [29] but he who blasphemes against the Holy Spirit never has forgiveness, but is subject to eternal condemnation."

Evil

An essential belief of Christianity is that God is in total control of everything, and yes, that even includes evil in the world. One of the more frequent questions among non-Christians is "If God is love, why does He allow evil in the world? Why do bad things happen to good people?" While that question is beyond the scope of this book (but very answerable), God's relationship to evil can best be illustrated by the story of Job (pronounced "Jobe") in the Old Testament. Job is considered to be one of the oldest books in the Bible.

The Bible tells us that Job was "blameless, upright, and one who feared God and shunned evil." The Bible says that one day the sons of God (many believe these were angels) came to present themselves to God, and Satan came with them. God asks Satan, "Have you considered my servant Job?" Satan responds that basically Job worships God because God blesses him and protects him (God in control). So, God removes the protection from Job and tells Satan that Job is within Satan's power. God is in control again.

Satan goes to work. Satan uses both foreign enemies to wipe out Job's livestock and violent storms to take out all of Job's sons and daughters, thus taking away everything that Job had except his health. Again, the sons of God and Satan present themselves to God, and God again asks Satan to consider His servant Job. God points out that Job had not sinned or turned away from God because of all that Satan had done. Now Satan responds that it is only because Job still has his health. So, God turns around and gives Satan power over Job's health. God points out that **Satan** cannot kill Job. God is still in control.

So, Job is stricken with painful boils all over his body. Job sits naked, wrapped in sackcloth, and sits among ashes. Interestingly, Job's wife then complains and questions Job about holding on to his integrity at this point. Literally, she tells him to "curse God and die."

These are only the first two chapters of Job. The book continues for forty more chapters, in which a conversation takes place between Job and his three visiting friends. In addition, God and Job have a conversation. In all of this, Job does not sin. In one of the more popular passages in the Bible, in Job, chapter 13, verse 15, Job concludes:

"Though He slay me, yet will I trust Him. Even so, I will defend my own ways before Him."

This Bible verse is one of the most powerful verses in the Bible. How could Job possibly still trust and believe in God? Somehow, Job knew God deeply. He had an intimate relationship with God and knew that God can do what God wants to do. He is God.

While Job could not possibly explain why these things had happened to him, he stayed steadfast, trusting that God would take care of him, if not in this life, then in the next. At the end of the book of Job, we find that not only did God fully restore Job, but He gave him twice as much as he had before. God is surely in total control of everything, including evil in the world.

No One Is Without Excuse

A big point of contention among non-believers is that everyone in the world couldn't possibly know about God. What about the people who live in the farthest, most remote regions and have little access to information or people, much less a Bible? "What about the people who live in the jungle?" is a common way to put it.

One of the things the Bible teaches is that God does not want anyone to perish but wants everyone to come to know Him. He loves everyone, and He sent Jesus to die for the whole world. How does this work? How can God want everyone to believe in Him when they are isolated, uneducated, and have never heard about Him? This is one of the reasons that Christians go on mission trips around the world, into the most remote places. I have been on these trips. On one particular trip, I went into the jungles of Malaysia and visited people in a village where they were practicing witchcraft and voodoo. Someone was coming to tell them what they did not know and had never heard. They were fortunate. But how about the ones that never see a guy like me?

The Bible says that no one is without excuse. The Bible says that God's invisible qualities can be seen in His creation and our world around us. Why is the sky blue? How does the weather change? What about the seasons of the year? How does that work? For those of us who live in the United States and have access to information and technology, we have a myriad of scientific resources that tell us how the world works. We, out of all the people on the earth, are surely without excuse. Here are two of the Bible passages for reference.

The 2nd book of Peter, chapter 3, verse 9:

9 The Lord is not slack concerning *His* promise, as some count slackness, but is longsuffering toward us, not willing that any should perish but that all should come to repentance.

In the book of Romans, chapter 1, verse 20:

20 For since the creation of the world His invisible *attributes* are clearly seen, being understood by the things that are made, *even* His eternal power and Godhead, so that they are without excuse.

The Bible

The Bible is the Word of God. It is the inspired, infallible Word of God and is the final authority and source of the Christian faith.

The 2nd book of Timothy, chapter 3, verses 16–17:

16 All Scripture *is* given by inspiration of God, and *is* profitable for doctrine, for reproof, for correction, for instruction in righteousness, 17 that the man of God may be complete, thoroughly equipped for every good work.

God

The Bible teaches that there is only one living, true, and eternal God who exists in three persons: God the Father, God the Son, and God the Holy Spirit. In the following passage from the Bible, Jesus has been praying for His disciples, and then He prays for all people who would believe in the future.

The book of John, chapter 17, verses 20–21:

[20] "I do not pray for these alone, but also for those who [a] will believe in Me through their word, [21] that they all may be one, as You, Father, *are* in Me, and I in You; that they also may be one in Us, that the world may believe that You sent Me."

Jesus

The Bible teaches that Jesus has existed eternally. At the right time in history, which the Bible describes as "the fullness of time," He was conceived by the Holy Spirit through the virgin Mary and was made Man. In this way, He is referred to as the Son of Man.

Holy Spirit

The Bible teaches that the Holy Spirit lives in those who genuinely believe in Jesus Christ. He seals their salvation. He helps the believer understand God's Word and know God. The Holy Spirit intercedes for the Christian, and, as the Bible says, He "groans" on behalf of the believer with prayers that we ourselves could not understand.

Baptism

Christians believe that baptism is the outward (public) sign of their faith and obedience. It emulates the death, burial, and resurrection of Jesus. True to biblical teaching, baptism is by submersion, following the example of John the Baptist and Jesus.

Gender, Marriage, and Sexuality

The Bible teaches that there are two genders, male and female. It also teaches that marriage is between one man and one woman. In addition, the Bible teaches that biblical sexual relations are reserved solely for the marriage covenant.

The Great Commission

Jesus' instructions to His followers were to go, share, and make disciples of all nations. Basically, Jesus was saying to go tell others about Him and share the Good News (the Gospel) of the forgiveness of sins and the promise of eternal life.

The book of Matthew, chapter 28, verses 16–20:

[16] Then the eleven disciples went away into Galilee, to the mountain which Jesus had appointed for them. [17] When they saw Him, they worshiped Him, but some doubted. [18] And Jesus came and spoke to them, saying, "All authority has been given to Me in Heaven and on earth. [19] Go therefore and make disciples of all the nations, baptizing them in the name of the Father and of the Son and of the Holy Spirit, [20] teaching them to observe all things that I have commanded you, and lo, I am with you always, *even* to the end of the age." Amen.

The Apostles' Creed

The Apostles' Creed is a statement of Christian faith, meant to provide clarity against false teachings and doctrine. It first appeared sometime between A.D. 250 and A.D. 340. It is believed that each of Jesus' Apostles contributed to it through their writings.[14] Today, various church denominations recite it regularly, like the Lutheran, Methodist, and Presbyterian churches, though that is changing.

> *I believe in God, the Father almighty,*
> *creator of Heaven and earth.*
>
> *I believe in Jesus Christ, his only Son, our Lord,*
> *who was conceived by the power of the Holy*
> *Spirit,*
> *and born of the Virgin Mary.*
> *He suffered under Pontius Pilate,*
> *was crucified, died, and was buried.*
> *He descended into Hell.*
> *On the third day, he rose again.*
> *He ascended into Heaven and is seated at the right*
> *hand of the Father.*
> *He will come again to judge the living and the*
> *dead.*
>
> *I believe in the Holy Spirit, the holy catholic*
> *Church,*
> *the communion of saints, the forgiveness of sins,*
> *the resurrection of the body, and the life*
> *everlasting. Amen.*[15]

---

[14] Paul Enns, *The Moody Handbook of Theology* (Chicago: Moody Publishers, 2008), 445, 704

[15] *Lutheran Book of Worship* (Minneapolis: Augsburg Publishing House, 1978), 85.

Chapter 10

Going Deeper: So, What Do I Talk About on Tuesday?

CONGRATULATIONS! If you are not a Christian, if you don't know what you believe, or if you are just skeptical, and you have gotten this far in reading this book, you are to be congratulated!

While I cannot fully understand the journey you are on, I can understand, having talked to thousands of non-Christians, how challenging it must be personally to explore something you have little or no knowledge about, particularly something that can be scary to consider and can invoke various emotions.

One of the most beautiful things about God and Christianity is that you are free to choose. As mentioned previously, *Christianity teaches that "free will" is a gift from God.* Everyone is free to choose what they believe or don't believe. God does not force anyone to believe in Him, and even more so, love Him. The gift of free will is something that sets us apart in all of creation. And, as I have mentioned previously, this book is all about sharing the very basics of Christianity and what the Bible says.

The only decision this book is intended for you to make is one that is conscientious and intentional. That decision can range anywhere from doing nothing and "not making any decision," to deciding that you are comfortable and firmly planted in exactly what you don't believe. You could decide to become a Christian. A decision can include doing nothing for now or deciding to explore more by reading the Bible. You could choose to search for more books like this one that can reinforce or introduce you to more about what the Bible says.

Again, the fact that you have read this book is an accomplishment. Hopefully, you have learned some things about Christianity and what the Bible says that will allow you to have a better conversation with your Christian and non-Christian friends. I encourage you to talk with both categories of friends in that regard. Asking questions to both types of friends about the things you have read in this book will generate great conversations. It will open opportunities to learn more and even deepen your relationships.

Personally, I have relationships where I have sat down with my non-Christian friends and had great conversations. It has taught me how to talk to people openly and honestly who have such different viewpoints. Even with someone I have just met, I have learned how to ask open-ended, non-threatening questions to get the conversation started.

A BIG piece of advice: It is important not to force your beliefs, or non-beliefs, for that matter, on the other person. Everyone needs to understand that a person is not going to "change their mind" in a matter of minutes over one conversation. It does not work that way (with any subject matter, really).

In these types of conversations, each party should gain the understanding that you are not going to come to a complete conclusion. I have observed this in my own personal conversations with others and had to learn to get comfortable with that fact. And, too, the next time I talked with that person, we would either pick it up from where we left off or start with a whole new topic. Either way, the conversation got rolling, and we had a robust talk. And after each get-together, there was always unfinished business. Both of us learned to be comfortable with that.

You do not have to understand it all. No one can understand it all. Just as I have mentioned here, the idea is to talk about the very basics of Christianity and what the Bible says. Believe me, there is so much more on what you have read about in each of the topics in this book. Hundreds of thousands of books and millions of words have been written on these topics. In the Christian world, the foundational books are called "Commentaries." Typically, they are written by biblical scholars, professors, and pastors around the world.

You do not have to "clean up your life." I have heard non-Christians say that they want to learn more about the Bible. Some even say they want to become a Christian someday, but first need to "clean up their life." This is not what the Bible teaches about becoming a Christian. *The Bible teaches that you just need to come as you are, in your current state.* We all come to the table as sinners. It is not that you are the one who will change yourself, but that after coming to faith in Jesus Christ, it is Jesus who will help you "clean up your life."

Here is what Jesus said in the book of Luke, chapter 5, from the New Living Translation (NLT):

[29] Later, Levi held a banquet in his home with Jesus as the guest of honor. Many of Levi's fellow tax collectors and other guests also ate with them. [30] But the Pharisees and their teachers of religious law complained bitterly to Jesus' disciples, "Why do you eat and drink with such scum?" [31] Jesus answered them, "Healthy people don't need a doctor—sick people do. [32] I have come to call not those who think they are righteous, but those who know they are sinners and need to repent."

How does this happen? The bottom line is that it is the work of the Holy Spirit that will guide you in how you will begin to live and what you will do next. Remember, in the previous chapter, I discussed the essential understanding that it is God the Father, through the Holy Spirit, who draws a person into becoming a believer.

When a person considers their life, where they are and where they are going, what they believe and what they don't believe, it all comes down to a matter of the heart. *What is really in a person's heart? What is in your heart?* What does your heart and soul believe, and for what does your heart and soul long?

Previously, I listed several reasons why people don't believe in God. Given that this book is supposed to be about a Monday conversation after reading my Sunday story, here is a list of what you could consider Tuesday's conversation to look like:

- ✓ There is no next step for me; I am glad I read this book.

- ✓ There is no next step for me; I am sorry I read this book.

- ✓ I will never become a Christian.

- ✓ I do not need to learn more about the Bible or Christianity.

- ✓ I still believe what I don't believe.

- ✓ I still believe what I don't believe, but am better informed.

- ✓ I still believe what I don't believe, but want to read more.

- ✓ I have questions.

- ✓ I have questions about my unbelief, questions about belief.

- ✓ I want to know more.

✓ I need to know more before I can decide to become a Christian.

✓ I want to become a Christian.

So, if you are in the camp of the first six categories, thank you for reading and finishing this book. I would love to hear from you! Please forward your confidential comments and feedback at https://www.dontcutthegrassonsunday.com. I hope it will not offend you if I tell you that I will be praying for you. ("You know how Christians are sometimes; we just have to do things like that.")

If you are one of the second six categories, you will be happy to know that a sequel is in the works. The proposed title is *Don't Cut the Grass on Sunday*, subtitle, *Going Deeper – A Tuesday Conversation for Non-Christians*. This book will break down the entirety of the Bible into seven topics:

1. Creation

2. Sin

3. Nation

4. Messiah

5. Church

6. Suffering

7. Return

For those of you who are in the category of "I want to become a Christian," did you know that you can do that now? Yes, you can do that right now, exactly where you are. Please understand, it is God Himself who is calling you, and it is His Holy Spirit working in you to offer this opportunity to become a Christian. I encourage you to simply bow your head, close your eyes, (get on your knees if you would like), and pray the following prayer:

Dear God, I know that I have done wrong things, and I now understand that I am a sinner and cannot save myself. I understand that apart from You, I can do nothing. I want to go to Heaven and be with You. Forgive me for my sin. I receive Jesus Christ as the sacrifice for my sin and want to receive Him as my Lord and Savior. It is in the name of Jesus Christ that I ask this. Amen!

If you prayed this prayer, get a Bible and start reading it (start with the book of John). Find a Bible-believing church, and talk to Christian friends you know to help get you engaged in a church or small group. Once you find a church, talk to them about what it means to get baptized and consider being baptized. Also, if you prayed this prayer, we would love to hear from you. Please send us a confidential email at https://www.dontcutthegrassonsunday.com.

XI. Books of the Bible

Old Testament

The Law

1. Genesis
2. Exodus
3. Leviticus
4. Numbers
5. Deuteronomy

History

6. Joshua
7. Judges
8. Ruth
9. 1 Samuel
10. 2 Samuel
11. 1 Kings
12. 2 Kings
13. 1 Chronicles
14. 2 Chronicles
15. Ezra

16. Nehemiah
17. Esther

Poetry

18. Job
19. Psalms
20. Proverbs
21. Ecclesiastes
22. Song of Solomon

Major Prophets

23. Isaiah

24. Jeremiah

25. Lamentations

26. Ezekiel

27. Daniel

Minor Prophets

28. Hosea

29. Joel

30. Amos

31. Obadiah

32. Jonah

33. Micah

34. Nahum

35. Habakkuk

36. Zephaniah

37. Haggai

38. Zechariah

39. Malachi

New Testament

The Gospels

40. Matthew

41. Mark

42. Luke

43. John

History

44. Acts

Letters

45. Romans

46. 1 Corinthians

47. 2 Corinthians

48. Galatians

49. Ephesians

50. Philippians

51. Colossians

52. 1 Thessalonians

53. 2 Thessalonians

54. 1 Timothy

55. 2 Timothy

56. Titus

57. Philemon

58. Hebrews

59. James

60. 1 Peter

61. 2 Peter

62. 1 John

63. 2 John

64. 3 John

65. Jude

Vision/Prophesy

66. Revelation

XII.   The Ten Commandments

Paraphrased from the New King James Version

1) You shall have no other gods before Me.

2) You should not have or make an idol for yourself.

3) You shall not take the name of the Lord your God in vain.

4) Remember the Sabbath day to keep it holy.

5) Honor your father and mother.

6) Do not murder.

7) Do not commit adultery.

8) Do not steal.

9) You should not give false testimony against your neighbor.

10) Do not covet your neighbor's possessions.

XIII. Selected Parables from the Bible

The Parable of the Sower is one of the parables in the Bible that Jesus both tells and explains. To give you an idea of how a believer reads and interprets it, I have shared my own understanding of what the parable means. Compare this with what the Bible actually says Jesus teaches. Christians who believe the Bible is the literal Word of God are not supposed to add to or take away from it, but I wanted to share how a Christian might explain it. God has given man a mind capable of understanding the Bible. How closely does my explanation align with Jesus'?

The Parable of the Sower (Matthew 13:1-9)

13 That same day, Jesus went out of the house and sat beside the sea. 2 And great crowds gathered about Him, so that He got into a boat and sat down. And the whole crowd stood on the beach. 3 And He told them many things in parables, saying: "A Sower went out to sow. 4 And as he sowed, some seeds fell along the path, and the birds came and devoured them. 5 Other seeds fell on rocky ground, where they did not have much soil, and immediately they sprang up, since they had no depth of soil. 6 But when the sun rose, they were scorched, and since they had no root, they withered away. 7 Other seeds fell among thorns, and the thorns grew up and

choked them. [8] Other seeds fell on good soil and produced grain, some a hundredfold, some sixty, some thirty. [9] He who has ears,[a] let him hear."

Author's Explanation

The Parable of the Sower describes how a person comes to true faith in Jesus Christ and receives eternal salvation in Heaven. The Sower represents God and His Holy Spirit, the seed is the Word of God, and the soil represents a person's position or condition in the world. Additionally, the Word of God may come to a person through reading the Bible or through another person sharing the gospel. The soil can describe state of a person's heart, or their "heart condition," meaning their openness and receptiveness to hearing about God.

The seed that falls along the path, where the birds immediately devour them, are the people who only hear or experience an inkling of the Word of God. The Word of God may come to these people, but some never really pay attention or hear it. The devil is instrumental in taking it away.

The seed that falls on the path, where the soil has no depth but immediately springs up, represents people who hear the Word, might understand a little, but quickly discount it. They dismiss it. In this instance, the "sun" could be peer pressure or cultural distractions that cause them to reject it.

The seed that falls among thorns, springs up, but is quickly choked out, represents those who hear the Word of God but allow the cares of the world to take priority. Things like money, careers, and relationships become more important and take precedence over the Word of God.

The seed that falls on good soil and produces grain manyfold is the Word of God that reaches an open, sincere, and receptive heart. The person receives the Word, studies the Word, and embraces the Word as a lifestyle. They understand it and make Jesus Christ the Lord and Savior of their lives.

The Parable of the Sower - Jesus's Explanation *Matthew 13:18-23*

[18] "Hear then the parable of the Sower: [19] When anyone hears the word of the kingdom and does not understand it, the evil one comes and snatches away what has been sown in his heart. This is what was sown along the path. [20] As for what was sown on rocky ground, this is the one who hears the word and immediately receives it with joy, [21] yet he has no root in himself, but endures for a while, and when tribulation or persecution arises on account of the word, immediately he falls away.[b [22] As for what was sown among thorns, this is the one who hears the word, but the cares of the world and the deceitfulness of riches choke the word, and it proves unfruitful. [23] As for what was sown on good soil, this is the one who hears the word and understands it. He indeed bears fruit and yields, in one case a hundredfold, in another sixty, and in another thirty."

The Parable of the Lost Son *(Luke 15:11-32, NKJV)*

[11] Then He said: "A certain man had two sons. [12] And the younger of them said to *his* father, 'Father, give me the portion of goods that falls *to me*.' So, he divided to them his livelihood. [13] And not many days after, the younger son gathered all together, journeyed to a far country, and there wasted his possessions with [d] prodigal living. [14] But when he had spent all, there arose a severe famine in that land, and he began to be in want. [15] Then he went and joined himself to a citizen of that country, and he sent him into his fields to feed swine. [16] And he would gladly have filled his stomach with [e] the pods that the swine ate, and no one gave him anything.

[17] "But when he came to himself, he said, 'How many of my father's hired servants have bread enough and to spare, and I perish with hunger! [18] I will arise and go to my father, and will say to him, "Father, I have sinned against Heaven and before you, [19] and I am no longer worthy to be called your son. Make me like one of your hired servants."'

[20] "And he arose and came to his father. But when he was still a great way off, his father saw him and had compassion, and ran and fell on his neck and kissed him. [21] And the son said to him, 'Father, I have sinned against Heaven and in your sight, and am no longer worthy to be called your son.'

[22] "But the father said to his servants, [f]'Bring out the best robe and put it on him, and put a ring on his hand and sandals on *his* feet. [23] And bring the fatted calf here and kill it, and let us eat and be merry; [24] for this my son was dead and is alive again; he was lost and is found.' And they began to be merry.

[25] "Now his older son was in the field. And as he came and drew near to the house, he heard music and dancing. [26] So he called one of the servants and asked what these things meant. [27] And he said to him, 'Your brother has come, and because he has received him safe and sound, your father has

killed the fatted calf.' [28] "But he was angry and would not go in. Therefore, his father came out and pleaded with him. [29] So he answered and said to *his* father, 'Lo, these many years I have been serving you; I never transgressed your commandment at any time, and yet you never gave me a young goat, that I might make merry with my friends. [30] But as soon as this son of yours came, who has devoured your livelihood with harlots, you killed the fatted calf for him.' [31] "And he said to him, 'Son, you are always with me, and all that I have is yours. [32] It was right that we should make merry and be glad, for your brother was dead and is alive again, and was lost and is found.'"

The Parable of the Lost Son Explained

The parable of the lost son is about God the Father's response toward us when we, as sinners, ask for forgiveness. God the Father can provide this response because of what Jesus did on the cross to offer this type of forgiveness. *It is about God's infinite GRACE toward us. Grace is unmerited favor,* something God offers that the Christian does not deserve and cannot do anything to earn. Jesus' obedience on the cross is what provides the means of GRACE.

While God is the focal point of the story, the main character appears to be the lost son. Even though we tend to focus on the lost son, the son who remains with his father helps us learn an important lesson as well.

The lost son is ready to move out, gain his independence, and see the world. He asks his father for his inheritance before he deserves it. In Jewish custom, the younger son would have received one-third of his father's entire inheritance, while the older son would receive two-thirds. Still, one-third would have been significant.

The father honors his youngest son's request, and off the son goes to live a life where he totally squanders it all in a short and fleeting period of time. When the younger son is at his lowest point mentally, emotionally, and physically, he comes to his senses and realizes what he has done (he has sinned). He reasons that if he asks for forgiveness and begs for a low position among his father's hired hands, his father will show him mercy. The younger son practices his big speech and heads back home.

However, before the son can even get home, his father sees him from a distance and responds with forgiveness and joy in his heart. The father clothes him and tells his servants to prepare food and set up a party to celebrate the youngest son's return.

Meanwhile, the older son hears about what has happened and is angry that his father has responded this way. When the father goes out to talk to his oldest son, the son tells him that in all the years he has been loyal, but has never been given a party like this one. The father responds and tells his oldest son that all he has is his, and that he has always been with him, basically, confirming and acknowledging his oldest son's loyalty. The father further explains that it is right to celebrate the younger son's return because he was lost and now is found. He was dead and is now alive. This is a true picture of how it is for us when we ask forgiveness from God and fully put our trust in Jesus for our salvation. As Christians, we too were once dead but now are alive in Christ.

The Parable of the Good Samaritan *Luke 10:25-37, NKJV*

25 And behold, a lawyer stood up to put Him to the test, saying, "Teacher, what shall I do to inherit eternal life?" 26 He said to him, "What is written in the Law? How do you read it?" 27 And he answered, "You shall love the Lord your God with all your heart and with all your soul and with all your strength and with all your mind, and your neighbor as yourself."

28 And He said to him, "You have answered correctly; do this, and you will live."

29 But he, desiring to justify himself, said to Jesus, "And who is my neighbor?" 30 Jesus replied, "A man was going down from Jerusalem to Jericho, and he fell among robbers, who stripped him and beat him and departed, leaving him half dead. 31 Now by chance a priest was going down that road, and when he saw him, he passed by on the other side. 32 So likewise, a Levite, when he came to the place and saw him, passed by on the other side. 33 But a Samaritan, as he journeyed, came to where he was, and when he saw him, he had compassion. 34 He went to him and bound up his wounds, pouring on oil and wine. Then he set him on his own animal and brought him to an inn and took care of him. 35 And the next day, he took out two denarii [b] and gave them to the innkeeper, saying, 'Take care of him, and whatever more you spend, I will repay you when I come back.'

36 Which of these three, do you think, proved to be a neighbor to the man who fell among the robbers?" 37 He

said, "The one who showed him mercy." And Jesus said to him, "You go, and do likewise."

The Parable of the Good Samaritan Explained

The Parable of the Good Samaritan, in its simplest form, is truly about what it means to be a good neighbor. However, we learn much more from the circumstances that Jesus presents in the story. First, Jesus was talking to a Jewish lawyer, and as we read, he wanted to justify himself and get confirmation that he was being a good person. So, Jesus sets up the story by including someone that Jews would not expect: the Samaritan. Jews and Samaritans did not like each other. In fact, they were enemies. The lawyer must have been surprised that it was a Samaritan who provided the act of kindness and mercy. Even so, the lawyer still knew, as his answer indicated, that it was the Samaritan who was the good neighbor.

The Other reason that this story is so important is that we learn that all the law and, really, all the Bible, can be summed up in two straightforward commandments. The first is, *"Love the Lord your God with all your heart, and all your soul, and all your strength, and all your mind."* The second is, *"Love your neighbor just as you love yourself."* Knowing and focusing on these two things as a Christian makes all the difference in the world.

The Rich Man and Lazarus *(Luke 16:19-31, NIV)*

[19] "There was a rich man who was dressed in purple and fine linen and lived in luxury every day. [20] At his gate was laid a

beggar named Lazarus, covered with sores, [21] and longing to eat what fell from the rich man's table. Even the dogs came and licked his sores.

[22] "The time came when the beggar died, and the angels carried him to Abraham's side. The rich man also died and was buried. [23] In Hades, where he was in torment, he looked up and saw Abraham far away, with Lazarus by his side. [24] So he called to him, 'Father Abraham, have pity on me and send Lazarus to dip the tip of his finger in water and cool my tongue, because I am in agony in this fire.'

[25] "But Abraham replied, 'Son, remember that in your lifetime you received your good things, while Lazarus received bad things, but now he is comforted here, and you are in agony. [26] And besides all this, between us and you a great chasm has been set in place, so that those who want to go from here to you cannot, nor can anyone cross over from there to us.'

[27] "He answered, 'Then I beg you, father, send Lazarus to my family, [28] for I have five brothers. Let him warn them, so that they will not also come to this place of torment.'

[29] "Abraham replied, 'They have Moses and the Prophets; let them listen to them.' [30] "'No, father Abraham,' he said, 'but if someone from the dead goes to them, they will repent.'

[31] "He said to him, 'If they do not listen to Moses and the Prophets, they will not be convinced even if someone rises from the dead.'"

Rich Man and Lazarus Explained

Jesus tells the story about the rich man and Lazarus in the presence of the Jewish leaders. The story is directed at them. Jesus is foreshadowing His death and resurrection, and the time when the Jewish leaders will hear about it and not believe. Jesus's reference to Moses and the Prophets is saying that the Jewish leaders have turned a blind eye to their teaching of a Messiah who would come to deliver the Jewish people.

Also, we learn quite a bit about Heaven and Hell in this story. One thing is that there will be a great chasm or barrier between the two places, and while the rich man can see Heaven, Lazarus apparently cannot see people in Hell. We learn that there will be great suffering in Hell, but comfort in Heaven. We learn that both the rich man and Lazarus are in an eternal place that cannot be changed.

We can also consider how we should live today. If we pursue the selfish pleasures of the world and give no consideration to relationships and others, then our reward is our life here on earth before death. However, if we understand that Jesus died for our sins and share this Good News with others, then we will enjoy an eternal resting home with God in Heaven.

The Parable of the Lost Sheep (Luke 15:1-7, NIV)

[1] Now the tax collectors and sinners were all gathering around to hear Jesus. [2] But the Pharisees and the teachers of the law muttered, "This man welcomes sinners and eats with them."
[3] Then Jesus told them this parable: [4] "Suppose one of you has a hundred sheep and loses one of them. Doesn't he leave the ninety-nine in the open country and go after the lost sheep until he finds it? [5] And when he finds it, he joyfully puts it on his shoulders [6] and goes home. Then he calls his friends and neighbors together and says, 'Rejoice with me; I have found my lost sheep.' [7] I tell you that in the same way

there will be more rejoicing in Heaven over one sinner who repents than over ninety-nine righteous persons who do not need to repent."

The Parable of the Lost Coin *(Luke 15:8-10, NIV)*

[8] "Or suppose a woman has ten silver coins and loses one. Doesn't she light a lamp, sweep the house, and search carefully until she finds it? [9] And when she finds it, she calls her friends and neighbors together and says, 'Rejoice with me; I have found my lost coin.' [10] In the same way, I tell you, there is rejoicing in the presence of the angels of God over one sinner who repents."

The Parable of the Lost Sheep and Lost Coin Explained

The Parable of the Lost Sheep and the Parable of the Lost Coin go together. Jesus tells these parables back-to-back because they share the same meaning. *There is joy and rejoicing in Heaven over even just one sinner who repents from sin and trusts in Jesus for their salvation.* In the parables, you and I are the lost sheep and the lost coin. Christians are the ones who realize their sin, turn from it, and receive Jesus as their Lord and Savior.

I once heard a story about the Parable of the Lost Sheep being told to tribesmen in an African village. When the story had finished, one of the tribesmen stood up and asked this question, "Wasn't God happy with the other ninety-nine?" What a great question! And the answer to the question is YES, absolutely God was happy with the other ninety-nine. Just like the older son in the Parable of the Prodigal Son, God is delighted with loyal and faithful followers. However, consider the shepherd who risked his life for just the one sheep. It demonstrates how God loves us and how much He is willing to pursue us in order that we might be saved. Similarly, consider how the woman who lost one coin must have worked to clean her house so that she could find that coin. Again, it demonstrates what God will do for us. He demonstrated it when He sacrificed His own Son, Jesus, to give us a way to repent and be saved.

The Parable of the Ten Virgins (Matthew 25:1-13)

[1] "At that time the kingdom of Heaven will be like ten virgins who took their lamps and went out to meet the bridegroom. [2] Five of them were foolish and five were wise. [3] The foolish ones took their lamps but did not take any oil with them. [4] The wise ones, however, took oil in jars along with their lamps. [5] The bridegroom was a long time in coming, and they all became drowsy and fell asleep.

[6] "At midnight, the cry rang out: 'Here's the bridegroom! Come out to meet him!'

[7] "Then all the virgins woke up and trimmed their lamps. [8] The foolish ones said to the wise, 'Give us some of your oil; our lamps are going out.'

[9] "'No,' they replied, 'there may not be enough for both us and you. Instead, go to those who sell oil and buy some for yourselves.'

[10] "But while they were on their way to buy the oil, the bridegroom arrived. The virgins who were ready went in with him to the wedding banquet. And the door was shut.

[11] "Later, the others also came. 'Lord, Lord,' they said, 'open the door for us!'

[12] "But he replied, 'Truly I tell you, I don't know you.'

¹³ "Therefore, keep watch, because you do not know the day or the hour."

The Parable of the Ten Virgins Explained

The Parable of the Ten Virgins is a story about being prepared. It is a message about being prepared for the second coming of Jesus to the earth and the day when He will establish His Kingdom here on earth. No one knows when that will be. The Bible does not tell us that. Also, it is the same with our own death; no one knows when they are going to die. So, if the Bible does not tell us when Jesus will return, what are we supposed to do? For Christians, it means to keep watch and be prepared.

Keeping watch is about awareness and includes looking out for the signs as the time grows nearer. These are called the signs of the end times, and the Bible does tell us about them. Because of advances in technology and communication, it is easier than ever to see them. Being prepared for Christians is about first making sure that Jesus is Lord of your life and that you are relying totally on His death and resurrection for your salvation. Also, it is about a Christian's "walk" in life, "walk" meaning one's lifestyle and spiritual wellness. A Christian who is truly watching and preparing for Jesus' return is likely reading their Bible regularly, praying regularly, and having fellowship with other Christians to learn and grow their faith.

XIV. Selected Notable People in the Bible

Old Testament

Adam & Eve:	The first man and the first woman created by God.
Cain & Abel:	The first sons of Adam and Eve. The first recorded murder in the Bible. Cain killed Abel.
Noah:	God asked Noah to build an Ark to prepare for the flood.
Shem, Ham, Japeth:	Noah's sons who were on the Ark with him.
Abraham:	God made a covenant with him and promised that he would be the father of a great nation (the Jewish nation).
Isaac:	Abraham's son, through whom God would fulfill His covenant with Abraham.
Jacob:	Isaac's son, through whom God would fulfill His covenant with Abraham. God changed Jacob's name to Israel.
12 Tribes:	The 12 tribes of Israel were the 12 sons of Jacob/Israel. They are Reuben, Simeon,

Ephraim, Judah, Dan, Naphtali, Gad, Asher, Issachar, Zebulun, Manasseh, and Benjamin. (Manasseh and Ephraim were sons of Joseph, and Levi's descendants were priests and did not own territory),"

Levi: Jacob/Israel's son, whose descendants were designated as priests.

Judah: Jacob/Israel's son, whose descendants would provide the Messiah, and His name is Jesus.

Joseph: Jacob/Israel's son, who would be sold into slavery in Egypt, and help grow and establish the Jewish nation.

Moses: From the tribe of Levi. Moses would lead the Israelite nation out of bondage, establish the Jewish law with God, and lead the people to wander in the desert for 40 years.

Joshua: Moses' successor who would lead Israel into the promised land.

Saul: The first King of Israel.

David: The second King of Israel. A man of war but a man after God's own heart. He would defeat the enemies of Israel and establish them in the promised land.

Solomon: David's son, who was the third King of Israel and considered the wisest man who ever lived. He ruled during the most peaceful and prosperous time in the nation's history.

Elijah: A great prophet of the Old Testament.

New Testament

John the Baptist:
: A great prophet of the New Testament. Prepared the way for Jesus' ministry through a message of repentance and baptism.

Jesus:
: The Son of God. The Messiah. The Savior of the World.

Mary:
: The mother of Jesus.

Joseph:
: Jesus' earthly father.

Disciples:
: Peter, Andrew, Philip, Thomas, John, Matthew, Simon, Bartholomew, James, Thaddeus, Thomas, Judas.

Thief- Cross:
: Name unknown. Asked Jesus to remember him in His kingdom.

Peter:
: Major contributor to starting the Church. Primarily carried the Gospel to the Jewish nation.

John:
: Major writer of the Gospel according to John. Also, he wrote the book of Revelation.

Stephen:
: The first Christian martyr.

Paul:
: Considered the great evangelist of the Gospel. Wrote much of the New Testament. Took the Gospel to the Gentiles.

XV.   Popular Bible Passages

- **John 3:16**

  "For God so loved the world that He gave His only begotten Son, that whoever believes in Him should not perish but have everlasting life."

- **Romans 8:28**

  "And we know that all things work together for good to those who love God, to those who are the called according to His purpose."

- **Psalm 51:10-12**

  [10] "Create in me a clean heart, O God, and renew a steadfast spirit within me.

  [11] Do not cast me away from Your presence, and do not take Your Holy Spirit from me.

  [12] Restore to me the joy of Your salvation, and uphold me by Your generous Spirit."

- **Romans 12:2**

  "And do not be conformed to this world, but be transformed by the renewing of your mind that you may prove what is that good and acceptable and perfect will of God."

- **Philippians 4:6-7**

  [6] "Be anxious for nothing, but in everything by prayer and supplication, with thanksgiving, let your requests be made known to God;

  [7] And the peace of God, which surpasses all understanding, will guard your hearts and minds through Christ Jesus."

- **Matthew 28:19-20**

  [19] Go therefore and make disciples of all the nations, baptizing them in the name of the Father and of the Son and of the Holy Spirit, [20] Teaching them to observe all things that I have commanded you; and lo, I am with you always, even to the end of the age. Amen."

- **2 Timothy 3:16-17**

  [16] "All Scripture is given by inspiration of God, and is profitable for doctrine, for reproof, for correction, for instruction in righteousness, [17] That the man of God may be complete, thoroughly equipped for every good work."

- **Hebrews 11:6**

  [6] "But without faith *it is* impossible to please *Him*, for he who comes to God must believe that He is, and *that* He is a rewarder of those who diligently seek Him."

- **2 Corinthians 5:21**

  [21] "For He made Him who knew no sin to be sin for us, that we might become the righteousness of God in Him."

- **John 14:6**

  "Jesus said to him, 'I am the way, the truth, and the life. No one comes to the Father except through Me.'"

- **Luke 2:11**

  "For there is born to you this day in the city of David a Savior, who is Christ the Lord."

- **John 1:5**

  "And the light shines in the darkness, and the darkness did not comprehend it."

- **2 Corinthians 12:9**

  "And He said to me, 'My grace is sufficient for you, for My strength is made perfect in weakness.' Therefore, most gladly I will rather boast in my infirmities, that the power of Christ may rest upon me."

- **Psalm 34:18**

  "The LORD *is* near to those who have a broken heart, and saves such as have a contrite spirit."

- **Matthew 6:31-34**

  [31] "Therefore, do not worry, saying, 'What shall we eat?' or 'What shall we drink?' or 'What shall we wear?' [32] For after all these things the Gentiles seek. For your heavenly Father knows that you need all these things. [33] But seek first the kingdom of God and His righteousness, and all these things shall be added to you. [34] Therefore, do not worry about tomorrow, for tomorrow will worry about its own things. Sufficient for the day is its own trouble."

- **Revelation 21:4**

  "And God will wipe away every tear from their eyes; there shall be no more death, nor sorrow, nor crying. There shall be no more pain, for the former things have passed away."

- **Romans 8:38-39**

  [38] "For I am persuaded that neither death nor life, nor angels nor principalities nor powers, nor things present nor things to come, [39] nor height nor depth, nor any other created thing, shall be able to separate us from the love of God which is in Christ Jesus our Lord."

- **John 15:13**

  "Greater love has no one than this, than to lay down one's life for his friends."

www.ingramcontent.com/pod-product-compliance
Lightning Source LLC
Chambersburg PA
CBHW071741120626
46550CB00002B/608